# THE HISTORICAL JESUS AND THE HISTORICAL JOSEPH SMITH

# THE HISTORICAL JESUS AND THE HISTORICAL JOSEPH SMITH

Tom Hobson

ELM HILL

A Division of
HarperCollins Christian Publishing

www.elmhillbooks.com

© 2019 George Thomas Hobson

## The Historical Jesus and the Historical Joseph Smith

Published in Nashville, Tennessee, by Elm Hill, an imprint of Thomas Nelson. Elm Hill and Thomas Nelson are registered trademarks of HarperCollins Christian Publishing, Inc.

Elm Hill titles may be purchased in bulk for educational, business, fund-raising, or sales promotional use. For information, please e-mail SpecialMarkets@ThomasNelson.com.

Biblical quotes, when they are not the author's own translation (which are marked with a *), are from the New King James Version. Copyright © 1982 by Thomas Nelson, Inc. Used by permission. All rights reserved. Sometimes, the author's translation coincides with that of the NRSV, and possibly others.

Quotes from the Book of Mormon are from the 1976 edition, copyright © 1963 by David O. McKay, Trustee-in-Trust for the Church of Jesus Christ of Latter-day Saints. All rights reserved. Quotes from the Doctrine and Covenants and Pearl of Great Price are from the 1973 edition, copyright © 1949 by George Albert Smith, Trustee-in-Trust for the Church of Jesus Christ of Latter-day Saints. All rights reserved.

Except for introductory materials found only in the print edition (copyright © 1971 by Deseret Book Company), quotes from Joseph Smith's History of the Church are in the public domain and may be found in their original handwritten manuscripts at https://www.josephsmithpapers.org/the-papers/histories/jspph3, accessed 6/20/2019.

Quotes from the Journal of Discourses are in the public domain.

### Library of Congress Cataloging-in-Publication Data

Library of Congress Control Number: 2019914710

ISBN 978-1-400329014 (Paperback)
ISBN 978-1-400329021 (eBook)

*This book is dedicated to my family: my wife Catherine, and our children Karen and Peter. I met Catherine in Oregon on the same 1977 youth group trip from St. Louis on which I met the Latter-day Saints in Utah. Our children grew up learning all they knew about the LDS people through cartoon books by Calvin Grondahl and Pat Bagley. The encouragement of my family makes this book their contribution to the spread of the Good News of God's grace as much as it is mine.*

# TABLE OF CONTENTS

# Just So You Know Where I'm Coming From…

I have had a heart for the Latter-day Saints for more than forty years. This book is the conversation I would love to have with any Latter-day Saint, or with any person who is thinking of becoming one. It contains all the reasons why I believe in Jesus, and why I do not trust Joseph. I have taken great care not to trash Joseph Smith, and I have tried my best to treat his claims with fairness. The way I conduct this conversation may lead some readers to mistakenly believe that I support the LDS faith, or that I believe the LDS faith to be an equally valid option alongside historic Christianity. Neither of these beliefs could be further from the truth! Ultimately, the undeniable facts about Joseph lead me to believe that he cannot be trusted to tell us the truth about God, while the undeniable facts about Jesus Christ lead me to believe that Jesus truly is who he claims to be, and that he is the only One who can put us right with God forever. Let's begin the conversation!

CHAPTER 1

# WHY WE MUST KNOW THE FACTS ABOUT JESUS AND JOSEPH

## Why Does It Matter?

Precisely who Jesus is, is absolutely central to the faith of the universal Church that believes in the God described in the Nicene Creed (Protestant, Catholic, and Orthodox). We're not just talking about his divine credentials. We're talking about exactly what he really said and did. If Jesus is not who the Gospels say he was, if they lied or made it up, we need not follow him. Examining and weighing the evidence we have is crucial. We must be sure that we know the facts about Jesus. Our eternity hangs in the balance.

Joseph Smith occupies a similarly pivotal place in the faith of the Latter-day Saints. He is not quite so central; no one believes Joseph to be God, or believes him to have died the atoning death that takes away our sins. But in LDS belief, following Joseph is central to whether a person joins the true Church of Jesus Christ.

In the LDS scripture *Doctrine and Covenants* 135:3, we read, "Joseph Smith, the Prophet and Seer of the Lord, has done more, save Jesus only, for the salvation of men in this world, than any other man who ever lived in it." That's pretty central!

Brigham Young announced on October 9, 1859, "Joseph Smith holds the keys of this last dispensation… no man or woman in this dispensation will ever enter into the celestial kingdom of God without the consent of Joseph Smith. From the day that the Priesthood was taken from the earth to the winding-up scene of all things, **every man and woman must have the certificate of Joseph Smith, Junior, as a passport to their entrance into the mansion where God and Christ are** – I with you and you with me. **I cannot go there without his consent.** He holds the keys of that kingdom for the last dispensation – the keys to rule in the spirit-world; and **he rules there triumphantly**… He reigns there as supreme a being in his sphere, capacity, and calling, as God does in heaven." (*Journal of Discourses* 7:289 – emphasis added)

While today's Latter-day Saints may not agree exactly with every word that Brigham Young says in the preceding sound bite, confirming one's belief that Joseph Smith is a prophet of God is an important part of any worthiness interview done to receive a temple recommend (permit to enter an LDS temple). "I testify that Joseph Smith is a prophet of God" is also a standard part of any testimony given from a pulpit in an LDS sacrament meeting. The question "Who is Joseph Smith?" must also be answered by any Christian or seeker who is sorting out the truth claims of both faith traditions. So it becomes just as important to know the facts about Joseph as it does for us to know the facts about Jesus.

Before I speak any further, I want to stop and make sure that our LDS friends are on board with Jesus, regardless of where the facts may lead about Joseph. If we can agree that Jesus Christ is the Savior and the One we must follow above all others, we can continue the conversation. If we do not agree that Jesus is more important than whatever we may conclude about Joseph, there is no need to continue the conversation. I am determined not to say or prove anything that would cause a Latter-day Saint to lose their faith in Jesus.

I want to be right about Jesus and about Joseph. If Jesus is not who I think he was, or if Joseph Smith is who his followers think he is, I am in big trouble. What I think about both leaders matters tremendously. I do not want to be caught dead believing a lie. While I do not follow Joseph, I take Joseph's claim to be a prophet with the utmost seriousness. Both the Latter-day Saint and I want to know the truth on these questions that determine our eternal destiny.

The truth about these two men is too important to be left to our own feelings or imaginations. Today, people want to believe that Jesus was all love and all inclusive, regardless of what the Gospels may say about him. There are all sorts of wildly different answers to the question "What Would Jesus Do?" Would Jesus have sex outside of marriage? Would Jesus use drugs? Would he go to war? We need facts, not wishful opinions. Many people project far too many of their own moral and political views onto Jesus. If our picture of Jesus doesn't shove us into our discomfort zone at times, it's not the real Jesus.

It is too easy to invent a Jesus who believes exactly what we do and lets us do whatever we want, a "Stepford Savior" who never contradicts us or gets in our way. Albert Schweitzer complained that scholars who wrote biographies of Jesus in his day were just gazing at their own faces in the bottom of a well; they told us more about themselves than they did about Jesus.

Contrary to what a large portion of today's world thinks, I am not free to make Jesus into whomever I want him to be. The same is true for Joseph Smith. Was Joseph truthful and honest? Did he keep the Word of Wisdom (see chapter 6)? Did he keep the law of chastity (see chapter 7)? What I think, doesn't matter; the facts are what they are, and my responsibility is to find and face those facts.

Let's not kid ourselves. I want to know the real Jesus, and the real Joseph. If Jesus or Joseph is from God, the facts will reveal that, and wishful thinking can't change that. Facts are all we have to prevent our biases and imaginations from sweet-talking us into self-delusion.

## How Can We Know the Facts?

None of us has direct access to human figures from the past. We cannot touch them in the flesh. We have no video or sound recordings. All we have is the traces or memories they leave behind, chiefly written records of oral testimony about them. Nevertheless, what we do have is enough to construct an adequate picture of what they said and did, enough to make the faith decisions we must make about Jesus and about Joseph.

Now at first, it hardly looks fair to compare the evidence we have on the life of Jesus versus the life of Joseph. With Joseph, we have an embarrassment of riches. We have the LDS scriptures that come from his hand. We have his diaries, much of the content of which was incorporated into his multi-volume *History of the Church*. In addition, we have truckloads full of personal and newspaper accounts from his contemporaries, both friends and enemies, about events from his life.

Because the earthly Jesus lived in a much more remote era, we have far less data to work with. We must remember: unlike Joseph, Jesus left us no writings. Aside from the canonical Gospels, all we have are a handful of disinterested references to Jesus and his followers from Greco-Roman sources (Josephus, Suetonius, Tacitus, Pliny), a few late references from rabid enemies of his (Celsus, the Talmud), and traditions from the early church, with not much reliable tradition that is not dependent upon the Gospels themselves. There are also the non-canonical gospels, but as we will see in chapter 3, these books flunk the criteria of authenticity that we must apply both to the Gospels and to Joseph.

How I wish that we had the kind of diary and newspaper evidence for Jesus that we have for the life of Joseph! But what we have about Jesus, I believe, is sufficient. We have enough on Jesus to know whether our facts are trustworthy. And what we have about Joseph can likewise be tested and weighed for veracity. We need not take the word of Joseph's enemies, if his friends or if he himself bears similar testimony. For both Jesus and Joseph, our evidence is as strong as we can expect from their time periods relative to our own.

Jesus scholars have developed their famous "criteria of authenticity" to identify portions of indisputable bedrock in the reported words and events from the life of Jesus. These criteria include the following:

**Multiple independent sources** – Skeptics have a difficult time dismissing a supernatural event like the Feeding of the 5000 that is found in all four Gospels, all with independent wording in the Greek originals. Granted, one wonders why only one of the seven famous sound bites of Jesus from the cross is recorded in more than one Gospel, but even this fact points to the independence of the four crucifixion accounts.

**Embarrassment** – Do friendly sources report unflattering information about Jesus? Ancient sources tend to omit details that make the hero of the story look bad. Why all four canonical Gospels tell us that an all-knowing Jesus chose a traitor for his inner circle must be because the facts compelled them to say so.

**Dissimilarity** – Does the information make Jesus stand out from his Jewish heritage and/or from the early church? The danger of pressing the criterion of dissimilarity too far in historical Jesus studies is that we end up with a Jesus who got nothing from his Jewish heritage, and left no impact on the early church! But neither can we assume that Jesus' views or behavior were just like those of his fellow Jews, or that the early church copied all of their teachings and practices straight from him. Areas where Jesus stands out as unique from both Judaism and the early church tend to be the places where we can be most confident of their historicity. The Golden Rule taught by Jesus (Matthew 7:12) is not unique; it is found in both Judaism and in pagan philosophy. But Jesus' rejection of divorce was unprecedented in Judaism, and the early church was already trying to soften it. Here is historical bedrock.

**Coherence** – Does the saying or event in question fit with the rest of what we know about Jesus? See chapter 3 on the question of whether Jesus advised his followers to buy swords to protect themselves, which does not seem to fit the non-violent character of the rest of Jesus' teaching (and yet for that very reason may be argued to be authentic).

**Rejection** – Do these words or events help explain why Jesus was arrested and crucified? The fact that Jesus goes around acting and talking like God would fit this criterion.

One or two of these criteria can be enough. There are plenty of rock-solid historical events from Jesus' life that are only recorded in one source, or do not trigger the criteria of embarrassment or dissimilarity. But the more of these criteria that are met for any saying or event in the Gospels, the stronger the likelihood that we are standing on historical bedrock.

Scholars who study the historical Jesus hold diverse perspectives. The so-called Jesus Seminar is famous for color coding the Gospels: red for material that they voted to be positively authentic, pink for likely, gray for doubtful, and black for absolutely false.[1] John Meier, author of a five-volume series on the historical Jesus called *A Marginal Jew*, believed that there were only four Gospel parables that were undoubtedly authentic parables of Jesus (!).[2]

But other scholars are much more confident about the authenticity of the Gospel accounts, and can show you exactly why. These include N. T. Wright,[3] Craig Blomberg,[4] Larry Hurtado,[5] and the authors of the volume *Key Events in the Life of the Historical Jesus*.[6] The bottom line is that the facts about the life of Jesus can withstand the most intense scrutiny of the most skeptical scholarship. I happen to accept all of what the four canonical Gospels tell us about Jesus, but even for those who are not committed to belief in the Bible, there is much that we can know for certain about the historical Jesus.

Some of the same criteria that are applied by scholars to the search for the historical Jesus can also be applied to Joseph Smith. Multiple sources are a better indication of historicity than one obscure comment in someone's diary. The criterion of embarrassment can be tremendously helpful, especially when details that are hard to believe are told by sources who would have had reason to omit or deny them. (On a few occasions, embarrassing details that are narrated in Joseph's diary are edited out when the events are reproduced in Joseph's *History of the Church*.) Even the criterion of rejection comes into play: Joseph's practice of plural marriage is not only found in multiple sources, but also helps explain why he was eventually killed.

Various biographies of Joseph resolve such questions about Joseph in different ways. In 2018, the LDS Church History Department released *Saints: The Standard of Truth*, a decidedly favorable treatment of Joseph.[7] At the other end of the spectrum are the works of Jerald and Sandra Tanner, exhaustively detailed but unfavorable to Joseph, including their self-published *Mormonism: Shadow or Reality?*[8] and *The Changing World of Mormonism*.[9]

In between these two perspectives are Fawn Brodie's *No Man Knows My History*[10] and Richard Bushman's *Joseph Smith: Rough Stone Rolling*.[11] Bushman's book is the most even-handed study of Joseph I can find from a sympathetic point of view. It gives the reader all the facts that both supporters and critics would want to know about Joseph. While you will want to read these expanded accounts of the facts on Joseph for yourself, my aim is to condense the sheer multitude of facts down to a limited number of the most convincing details. These will help us arrive at conclusions that will guide our decisions about Joseph and whether he is God's chosen prophet who can point us to the real Jesus.

---

[1] See Robert W. Funk, *The Five Gospels: The Search for the Authentic Words of Jesus*, New York: Macmillan, 1993.

[2] John Meier, *A Marginal Jew* (New Haven/London: Yale University Press, 2016), 5:210.

[3] N. T. Wright, *The New Testament and the People of God*, Minneapolis: Fortress, 1992; *The Resurrection of the Son of God*, Minneapolis: Fortress, 2003.

[4] Craig L. Blomberg, *The Historical Reliability of the Gospels*, Downers Grove: IVP Academic, 2007.

[5] Larry Hurtado, *Lord Jesus Christ: Devotion to Jesus in Earliest Christianity*, Grand Rapids: Eerdmans, 2003.

[6] Darrell L. Bock and Robert L. Webb, eds., *Key Events in the Life of the Historical Jesus*, Grand Rapids: Eerdmans, 2010.

[7] Church of Jesus Christ of Latter-day Saints, *Saints: The Story of the Church of Jesus Christ in the Latter Days. Volume 1: The Standard of Truth, 1815-1846*, Salt Lake City: Intellectual Reserve, 2018. Referred to throughout this book as *Saints: The Standard of Truth*.

[8] Jerald and Sandra Tanner, *Mormonism: Shadow or Reality?*, Salt Lake City: Modern Microfilm, 1972.

[9] Jerald and Sandra Tanner, *The Changing World of Mormonism*, Chicago: Moody, 1980.

[10] Fawn M. Brodie, *No Man Knows My History*, 2nd edition, New York: Alfred A. Knopf, 1977.

[11] Richard Lyman Bushman, *Joseph Smith: Rough Stone Rolling*, New York: Vintage, 2005.

When putting together a puzzle, the person who gets the puzzle right is the person who uses all the pieces. Likewise, the truest picture of Jesus or of Joseph is the one that correctly uses all the pieces available to us. In the cases of both Jesus and Joseph, it is extremely important that we get the picture right. Our eternal future hangs on whether we correctly assess who they are and where they lead us.

## But What Good Is Evidence?

Yet all the evidence in the world cannot change the mind of a person who refuses to see evidence for what it is. We all tend to see evidence the way we want to, based on our own preconceived biases. It's like the story of the mental patient who was convinced that he was dead. The therapist uses medical books and films of autopsies to eventually convince the patient, "Dead people don't bleed." Immediately, the therapist stabs the patient in the hand with a scalpel. The patient looks down at his bleeding hand and cries, "Dead people do bleed after all!"

For many Latter-day Saints, the testimony of the Holy Ghost in their hearts overrules any amount of evidence one might share with them to persuade them to change their belief. Moroni 10:4 in the Book of Mormon says that if we ask God whether the book's message is true, "he will manifest the truth of it unto you, by the power of the Holy Ghost." Likewise, the Protestant Westminster Confession of Faith (1:5) says that "our full persuasion and assurance of the infallible truth and divine authority [of the Bible] is from the inward work of the Holy Spirit, bearing witness by and with the Word in our hearts." Both traditions teach that the testimony of the Spirit is the ultimate confirmation of God's truth.

So, what good is historical evidence for Jesus, or for Joseph? The answer is: evidence and Spirit must go hand in hand. God's Spirit cannot authenticate a falsehood. The role of God's Spirit is to open our eyes to see the truth for what it is. The role of evidence is to give us reasons why we should trust a testimony to Jesus or Joseph, and not the testimony of countless Muslims or Hindus to their very different claims of truth.

But why is historicity so important in our search for God's truth? Does it really matter whether events in the Bible, such as the accounts in the Gospels, really and truly happened? Likewise, does it matter whether the details we have heard about the life and teachings of Joseph Smith are solid fact? Yes, fiction and legend can sometimes serve as artful expressions of truth. But both the Bible and LDS faith are based on factual claims. Heads roll at the news department when news reports are found to be fiction. Similarly, the claim that Jesus rose from the dead loses its value if Jesus is still in the ground, and the risen Jesus becomes no different than sightings of Elvis. (Search online for my series, "Historicity: Does It Matter?" in the *Presbyterian Outlook*.)

Truth cannot be based on feelings. Proverbs 14:12* (= 16:25) says, "There is a way that seems right to a person, but its end is the way to death." Feelings are what led John F. Kennedy Jr. to believe that he was flying on a level course on that fateful night of July 16, 1999, when in reality he and his passengers were plunging straight downward to their death. The instruments in his cockpit told a different story than his feelings.

Our feelings are notoriously unreliable. When considering the claims of Jesus, Joseph, or even Muhammad, testimony is no substitute to the tests of a prophet that the Bible gives us. The first test is the prophet's lifestyle: "You will know them by their fruits" (Matthew 7:16) – not the fruits of their followers, but the lifestyle of the prophet himself. The second test is whether the prophet is a truth teller. Do his prophecies come true? (Deuteronomy 18:20-22) Does the prophet teach the truth about God? (Deuteronomy 13:1-5)

A prophet cannot afford to be a deceiver or dishonest. Prophets may be human and may be mistaken on questions like medical science (a subject where science itself is still learning and correcting itself about what we thought we knew). But a prophet must be reliable where it really counts. If a prophet lies about what happened yesterday, how can we trust him to tell us the truth about God? The risk is that if we follow a false prophet, we are in danger of going where that prophet goes.

Back in 1978, the morning after we heard the news that Jim Jones and his 900 followers had committed mass suicide, when I came to class at college that morning, my professor (who was an agnostic) asked me, "Tom, how in the name of **God** [emphasis original] do you explain what just happened?" My response was, "It proves that it is possible to be sincerely – wrong." And in this particular case, the price of being wrong was sky-high.

May the Holy Ghost open our eyes and hearts to see the truth for what it is as we examine the evidence on the lives of the historical Jesus and the historical Joseph.

# CHAPTER 2

# HISTORICAL BEDROCK IN THE LIFE OF JESUS

What can we know absolutely for certain about the life of Jesus, regardless of whether or not we believe in the accuracy of the Bible? Based on the historian's "criteria of authenticity" identified in the previous chapter, let's take a look at some of the events and overall themes from the life of Jesus for which there is the strongest evidence.

**Examples of Historical Bedrock**

All four Gospels make a huge connection between Jesus and John the Baptist. James Dunn calls John "the inescapable preface to Jesus." The historian Josephus (*Antiquities* 18:116-19) pays more attention to John than he does to Jesus: he writes 163 words in Greek about John, versus possibly eighty about Jesus, depending on how much of the famous passage about Jesus in *Antiquities* 18:63-64 is authentic. In fact, we need to answer the question whether or not the Gospels have exaggerated the connection between John and Jesus, and whether John's endorsement of Jesus is historical, or whether it is an invention of the early church to try to hitch their wagon to John's popularity.

Despite these potential objections, Jesus' baptism by John meets both the criteria of multiple sources and embarrassment. Three sources record the actual baptism (John technically does not). And together, the four canonical Gospels tie John and Jesus together in such a way as to make Jesus look like a follower or at least someone who endorses John, a move that could potentially send the wrong message about who is greater, John or Jesus.

Blomberg writes on the historicity issue: "Given the early Christian concern to play down the role of John the Baptist and to exalt Jesus, just about everything that places John in a positive light is likely to be historical…"[1] In Matthew 11:11 and Luke 7:28, Jesus credits John with being the greatest human who ever lived up till then (including Abraham and Moses). Jesus even says that John is the Elijah predicted by Malachi (Matthew 11:14). Such high praise for John by Jesus is unlikely to have been invented.

Matthew is the only Gospel that says John tries to prevent Jesus from being baptized. John reflects the mixed feelings of Matthew's audience. The Gospel of the Hebrews (quoted in Jerome, *Against Pelagius* 3:2) has Jesus object: "How have I sinned, that I should go and be baptized by him, unless perhaps this very thing I have said is a sin of ignorance?" Blomberg argues, "Because of the theological problems created by Jesus accepting John's baptism that symbolized repentance of sin, it is inconceivable that the early church would have created this story."[2] The connection between Jesus and John is historical bedrock.

---

[1] Craig L. Blomberg, *Jesus and the Gospels: An Introduction and Survey* (2nd edition; Nashville: Broadman and Holman, 2009), 257.

[2] Blomberg, *Jesus*, 259.

Jesus' cleansing of the Temple is an event that even the Jesus Seminar concedes to be historical. Could this be an invention that contradicts the real Jesus, invented by a detractor to make him look bad? Or is this a shocking exception in the life of Jesus that proves the rule? It appears to be an unforgettable memory, a fact that could not be suppressed even if someone tried. This event seems to play a major role in Jesus' eventual arrest and execution.

One confusing fact is that, although all four Gospels testify to this event, John puts it near the beginning of Jesus' ministry, while the Synoptic Gospels put it at the end. One could argue that John is using the editorial license of a filmmaker, one could declare one or the other version to be in error, or one could imagine that Jesus pulls this move twice: the first time, he gets blown off, while the second time, the authorities take action. One piece of evidence in favor of an early Temple cleansing is where the Jews say in John 2:20 that they've been building the Temple for "forty-six years." Since Herod started the reconstruction in 20 BC, that would make the current date 26 AD, right at the beginning of Jesus' ministry (according to the formula given in Luke 3:1-2). Here in John 2:19, Jesus also says "Destroy this temple, and in three days I will raise it up," a line that comes back garbled at Jesus' trial – it may have been three years since Jesus first uttered those words. Only in John does Jesus make a whip, drive out the cattle and sheep, and tell the dove sellers to take them away. The Scriptures quoted in John and the Synoptic Gospels are different, so the witnesses are independent. And all four Gospels agree that the issue is authority.

If this event was not historical, then why was it created, unless it was created by enemies (in which case, why did all four Gospels include it?)? No one in Scripture explains why Jesus did it, or draws any theological conclusions from it. Jesus seems to care about the Temple a lot more than the early church did. John explains via Scripture that zeal for God's house prompted Jesus' action. Mark 11:16 tells us that Jesus would not even allow anyone to carry loads through the temple. And the violence that Jesus uses here on Temple grounds is unprecedented!

The criterion of embarrassment applies to this event. The early church needed to avoid the impression that Jesus (or they themselves) were troublemakers. Rome saw itself as a defender of temples, and Jesus appears to be attacking those who ran the Temple. So why would the church have created such an event that makes Jesus look dangerous?

Much discussion revolves around Jesus' words about destroying this temple (who in the early church would make that up?). But driving out those who were ruining the sanctity of the Temple is far different from wanting to destroy it. Jesus viewed the Temple as being the holiest place on earth (although he refers to himself in Matthew 12:6 as "greater than the Temple").

One valid question is: How could Jesus police everyone in a busy thirty-five-acre Temple court? And how could Jesus create a disturbance, without the Temple guard and the Roman soldiers next door quickly taking action? The Romans probably did not see a problem – no one was provoking them. And the authorities may not have taken action because they feared the people.

If we don't believe that Jesus actually commanded that much support, remember: everyone agrees that Jesus was arrested at night, specifically in the absence of the crowds. So if we ask how Jesus could police everyone, the answer is easy, if the multitudes regarded him as a prophet, like John. And Jesus could easily prevent people from coming into the courtyard, since most came in from one direction. The rabbis in the Mishnah (Berakoth 9:5) forbid using the Temple courtyard for a shortcut. Jesus seeks to enforce this.

What Jesus was so angry at is far from clear. All we have is his splicing together of Isaiah 56:7 and Jeremiah 7:11 in the Synoptic Gospels ("Is it not written, My house shall be called a house of prayer for all nations? But you have made it a den of robbers!"), and his allusion to Zechariah 14:21 in John 2:16* ("Stop making my Father's house a house of trade!"). Jesus seems to be fulfilling the prophecy of Malachi 3:14 that God will come to his temple to judge and purify it, yet no one in the New Testament cites this prophecy.

Jesus seems to be mad at the moneychangers. Did he object to the pagan Tyrian shekel that was required for the Temple tax (to which other coins had to be converted)? Why would he object? All silver coins had pagan mottos and images on them. Was he protesting the Temple tax? That tax was a direct command of the Torah, and Jesus himself pays it in Matthew 17:24-27. Perhaps it was the exorbitant exchange rate charged by the money changers, but that is just a guess.

Jesus seems to be angry at the sellers of sacrificial animals (he drives out both buyers and sellers). There are two issues here. First, there is the racket on approved merchandise. You could bring your own animal to sacrifice, but then the priests could refuse to accept it because they find some blemish in it, "But buy one of ours, and ours are guaranteed." Priests can then drive up the price, even on pigeons (which were all that the poor could afford). The other issue is where this is being done. Until recently, all sacrifices in town were bought in a market on the Mount of Olives. Caiaphas and his cronies appear to have recently started their own market in the Temple courtyard itself. That may be what gets Jesus the angriest.

And that may be the very issue that sets the match to the gasoline with the chief priests over what Jesus has done. In all four Gospels, the result of what Jesus does is a demand to know by what authority he is acting. "Just who do you think you are?" It is a question that begs an answer. This event fits the criteria of multiple independent sources, embarrassment, dissimilarity, rejection, all but possibly coherence. Like it or not, no one can deny this historical bedrock from the life of Jesus!

The Last Supper is an event that gives us multiple independent sources, including Paul (writing in 1 Corinthians 11:23-25 in 55 AD), plus we have the criterion of dissimilarity with Judaism; we have a Passover, but a radical reinvention of it. Eating someone's body and blood is as un-Jewish as you can get! True, there is no dissimilarity with the early church, but are we supposed to believe that the early church made this sacrament up out of thin air? Isn't it far more likely that they got this from Jesus? One can argue that all Jesus did was break the bread and pass the cup, but that it was the church who put the meaning on those elements after the cross. But again, where did the church get these meanings, if not from Jesus? If it wasn't Jesus, then somebody in the church deserves the Nobel Prize for theology! But how could a bunch of pretenders come up with such powerful ideas?

Jesus seems to have made advance reservations for where to eat the meal; since everything in Jerusalem gets booked up, Jesus doesn't want a repeat of what happened when he was born. He tells the disciples they will meet a man carrying a jar of water, who will lead them to the right place. (Look for a guy pushing a baby carriage – you'll only see one, and you can't mistake him for anyone else.) The dining room is a *katalyma*, the same word for the place where there was no room in Bethlehem ("guest room" rather than "inn").

Where was this room? Israeli tours will take you to a simple modern room at a high point in the southwestern part of the Old City. This structure is built over a first-century stone foundation that appears to be the earliest Christian synagogue, a worship site which faces Calvary, not the Temple.

For Jesus' words at the supper, we have Matthew, Mark, Luke, and Paul, plus for the prayers used for the Supper by the early church, we have the *Didachē* (95 AD). A key item of debate is whether or not Jesus says in Luke "which is given for you; do this in remembrance of me." These words are in Paul, but are missing from Manuscript D and some Latin copies of Luke. Sadly, the word "broken" we often hear is in very few ancient manuscripts (only the Syriac and Old Latin versions of 1 Corinthians read "broken for you"). The saying about the cup is either "This is my blood of the covenant" (Mark) or "This cup *is* the new covenant in My blood" (Paul, Luke). The mention of forgiveness of sins is only found in Matthew. "Poured out" seems to be only in Mark and Matthew. The witnesses are independent, but together, they confirm that this was no invention to explain some practice of the early church.

## Miracles: More Historical Bedrock!

As a group, the miracles of Jesus offer strong evidence of historicity. According to one count, the canonical Gospels give us accounts of at least six exorcisms, seventeen healings (including three resurrections), and eight nature miracles, plus countless more acts that are merely alluded to, like the seven demons cast out of Mary Magdalene (Luke 8:1).

In the 90's, Josephus (a non-Christian) testifies to Jesus' reputation as a man of "extraordinary deeds" (*paradoxōn ergōn*). The Talmud (based on tradition going back to at least the second century) charges Jesus with sorcery: "On Passover Eve they hanged Yeshu of Nazareth, who practiced sorcery, incited and led Israel astray." (Sanhedrin 43a) Even scholars such as Marcus Borg admit that the echoes of Jesus' miracle-working power outside the church are too strong to dismiss.

Remember John Meier, the scholar who argues that only four of Jesus' parables are undoubtedly genuine (see Chapter 1)? This same scholar makes a passionate case that Jesus truly performed miracles.[3] He says the single most important piece of evidence is the "*multiple attestation of sources and forms... As for multiple sources, the evidence is overwhelming. Every Gospel source (Mark, Q, M, L, and John), every evangelist in his redactional summaries, and Josephus to boot affirm the miracle-working activity of Jesus...some do it repeatedly.*"[4] Meier also argues that the early dating of this literary testimony "is almost unparalleled for the period."[5] Jewish heroes like Honi the Circle Drawer and Hanina ben Dosa, and pagan miracle-workers like Apollonius of Tyana, get miracles attributed to them only 200 years later or more, not forty years or less. And nowhere else do we find such a combination of popular preacher + authoritative teacher of morality + miracle-worker. Meier writes, **"if the miracle tradition from Jesus' public ministry were to be rejected *in toto* as unhistorical, so should every other Gospel tradition about him"** (emphasis added).[6]

Jesus' miracles are different than the kinds we find in Jewish and pagan healing stories of his day. While Jews use prayers and pagans use magic instruments, Jesus almost always does the miracle himself without calling on anyone else, and only in three cases does he use a healing aid such as mud or saliva. He never uses long incantations or magic words, and never does anyone coerce Jesus to do a healing, nor does Jesus try to coerce God into miracles. Unlike magicians, Jesus never heals paying customers, and never performs miracles that hurt or punish.

Jesus' miracles often feature specific eyewitness details. The widow at Nain whose son is raised from the dead (Luke 7:11-17) is unnamed, but three miracle recipients are named: Lazarus (John 11:1-44), Jairus = *Ya'ir* (the synagogue leader whose daughter Jesus raises from the dead – Matthew 9:18-26 = Mark 5:21-43 = Luke 8:40-56), and Bar-Timaeus = *Bar-Timai*, the blind man at Jericho (Matthew 20:29-34 = Mark 10:46-52 = Luke 18:35-43). On occasion, we get Aramaic sound bites from Jesus: in the raising of Jairus' daughter, he says *Talitha, qumi!* ("Fawn, arise!"), while to the deaf/mute man in Mark 7:31-35, he says, *Ephphatha!* ("Be opened!")

Mark 8:22-25 even records a healing of an unnamed blind man where Jesus has to try twice (on Jesus' first try, the patient says, "I see people, but they look like trees walking"*), an account that fits the criterion of embarrassment so well that neither Matthew nor Luke includes the incident. Who would invent such detail? And who would have invented the detail that Jesus did not know who touched him when he heals the woman with the twelve-year hemorrhage (Mark 5:30-33)? Even the disciples can't see why Jesus would ask such a question. Details like these are what we would expect from reliable eyewitness testimony.

---

[3] Meier, *Marginal Jew*, 2:619-631.

[4] Meier, *Marginal Jew*, 2:619 (emphasis original).

[5] Meier, *Marginal Jew*, 2:624.

[6] Meier, *Marginal Jew*, 2:630.

We've looked at just a few events that qualify as historical bedrock in the life of Jesus. Now, let's take a look at his teachings. What can we be absolutely sure that Jesus taught?

## Trademark Jesus Language

Two expressions are part of Jesus' distinctive way of speaking (what Larry Hurtado calls his "idiolect"). One is his use of the term "Son of Man." Early Christians faithfully preserve Jesus' Son of Man sayings, but (with the exception of once by Stephen) they almost never use this expression themselves, especially not after we get to the second century AD. In fact, the Greek expression (literally "the son of the man") is not found once in the Greek Old Testament among the dozens of times the phrase "son of man" occurs in the Hebrew; it seems to have been constructed specifically for use in quoting Jesus.

"Mammon" is a positive word to the rabbis of Jesus' day. Only in Jesus do we see "the unusual and imaginative use of this common Aramaic word to depict a demonic force or false god pitted against the true God."[7]

The other expression unique to Jesus is his "Amen, Amen [Verily, verily], I say to you." Only Jesus uses this expression; not the Jews, not the early church. The double Amen is found only in John (twenty-five times), but "Amen, I say to you" is found fifty-one times in Matthew, Mark, and Luke.

Jesus also talks about the "kingdom of God / Heaven" more than any other Jewish teacher of his day (approximately eighty-five times). Not being a guy who could write a whole book on the subject, I will not attempt to unpack exactly what the term meant to Jesus, but in the Gospel of John, with very few exceptions, "kingdom of God" gets replaced by "eternal life." In fact, in John 3:3, Jesus says, "Unless someone is born anew, he cannot see the kingdom of God," but then Jesus replaces his "kingdom of God" language with "eternal life" by the time he gets to 3:16. And the few times that Paul uses "kingdom of God," he seems to be almost quoting otherwise unknown sayings of Jesus, such as "those who practice such things shall not inherit the kingdom of God" (Galatians 5:21*, similarly 1 Corinthians 6:10, Ephesians 5:5), and "the kingdom of God is not food and drink" (Romans 14:17*).

Jesus' teachings about the kingdom of God refer to it as being both future and right now. The kingdom of God refers to that glorious future when God's rule defeats Satan once and for all, and where those who have been rescued from sin by the mercy of God will live with God forever. But it also refers to God's arrival on earth during the earthly lifetime of Jesus, breaking the power of the evil one right now, and filling God's people with the power of the Holy Ghost. Jesus keeps that kingdom front and center in his preaching. It is trademark Jesus language.

## Tough on Sin, Amazing Love for Sinners

If there's one evil the historical Jesus couldn't stand, it was hypocrisy. All thirteen times the word *hypokritēs* (hypocrite) is used in the New Testament, we find it in the mouth of Jesus, mainly clustered in the Sermon on the Mount and in Matthew 23. The related noun *hypokrisis* (hypocrisy) is used six times, half of them by Jesus. In these passages, Jesus complains about phoniness in giving, prayer, and fasting, all practices where it's easy to pretend or make a show of religiosity. Jesus also uses the word to describe those who point the finger at others' sins while they are blind to their own (Matthew 7:5) and those who criticize him for breaking rabbinic tradition while they themselves excuse the breaking of God's law (Matthew 15:7 = Mark 7:6). Jesus also uses the word to refer to the "pretenders" who asked him whether they should pay taxes to Caesar (Matthew 22:18).

Jesus is passionately opposed to phonies, play-actors (the root meaning of *hypokritēs*), and pretenders. Jesus

---

[7] Meier, *Marginal Jew*, 3:518.

wants people who are what they claim to be, people who do what they say (Matthew 23:3). He warns his followers to beware of the "hypocrisy" of the Pharisees, saying, "Nothing is covered up that will not be revealed, and nothing secret that will not become known. Therefore whatever you have said in the dark will be heard in the light, and what you have whispered in inner rooms will be proclaimed from the housetops." (Luke 12:1-3*) Jesus wants people who can be trusted, whose word is more dependable than an oath (Matthew 5:33-37).

But while the historical Jesus was tough on sin, there is strong evidence that he also showed unprecedented love for sinners. Concerning Jesus eating with tax collectors and harlots, Blomberg says, "apparently few in either religion [Judaism or the early church] dared emulate Jesus' scandalous disregard for appearances in dining with these overtly immoral groups, so neither Jew nor Christian is likely to have made up such a description of Jesus."[8] Once again, here we are on historical bedrock. The huge issue for us in the twenty-first century is whether Jesus condoned the sinful lifestyles of these groups, as is claimed by today's progressives.

Actual evidence does not allow us to imagine that Jesus gave Zacchaeus permission to continue practicing extortion. Nor did Jesus excuse the woman caught in adultery. One is on much firmer ground to argue that Jesus' approach to the tax collectors and hookers would have been like John the Baptist's (see Luke 3:10-14). When Jesus is dining at Levi's house, it says there were many who "followed" him (Mark 2:15); one could argue this means "follow" in an obedience sense rather than a crowd-groupie sense.

Despite modern attempts to invent a permissive Jesus, all of the actual evidence points to an historical Jesus who was a Puritan on sexual morality. We see this from his teaching that "whoever looks at a woman in order to desire her [King James: "lust after her," but the word is a generic word for both good and bad desires] has already committed adultery with her in his heart." (Matthew 5:28*) We also see that Jesus is far from permissive in his strict teaching on divorce, which is confirmed by the historical criteria of multiple independent witnesses (Matthew 5:31-32, Matthew 19:6-9, Mark 10:2-12, Luke 16:18), dissimilarity (it contradicted Judaism, and the early church tried to soften it), and embarrassment (even in Matthew 19:11, the disciples hit the panic button here). Whether we choose to take Jesus' words as an absolute prohibition, or whether we understand them as simply a reminder that we cannot erase a sexual relationship, Jesus' teaching about divorce is as historically bedrock as it gets. Taking both teachings together, how can we argue for a permissive Jesus who utters such strict teachings?

Jesus' teaching on divorce is tied to the Torah's declaration "The two [a man and a woman] shall become one flesh" (Genesis 2:24), words that are reaffirmed twice by Jesus (Matthew 19:4-6, Mark 10:7-8) and twice by Paul (1 Corinthians 6:16, Ephesians 5:31). Jesus affirms the Bible's central teaching on sexuality: sex is only for lifelong loving marriage between a man and a woman. If Jesus disagreed with the Torah and mainstream Judaism on sexual morality, his teaching on divorce was proof that he had the courage to speak up and say so.[9]

That goes also for the question of whether Jesus was OK with same-sex intimacy. It is commonly argued (as Jimmy Carter does) that Jesus did not speak one word on the subject. But Jesus clearly affirms sex only between a man and a woman. Furthermore, on Jesus' sin list in Mark 7:21-22, Jesus names not only fornication (*porneia*) and adultery (*moicheia*), but also the sin of *aselgeia*, translated "lasciviousness" in the King James Version and "lewdness" or "licentiousness" in other versions. The word refers to shocking sexual behavior beyond mere fornication or adultery. I have made the case that it was Jesus' term for same-sex intimacy.[10] If I am correct, the evidence would

---

[8] Craig L. Blomberg, "The Authenticity and Significance of Jesus' Table Fellowship," in Bock and Webb, eds., *Key Events*, 237.

[9] Meier, *Marginal Jew*, 3:503: "In a sense, one could call both Jesus and the Essenes extreme conservatives… apart from the two special cases of divorce and celibacy, where he diverged from mainstream Judaism, his views *were* those of mainstream Judaism." (Emphasis original)

[10] G. Thomas Hobson, "*Aselgeia* in Mark 7:22," *Filologia Neotestamentaria* 21 (2008): 65-74. Available online, or in a non-technical version

still be slim, but the criterion of coherence applies (it fits with Matthew 19:4-6 and Mark 10:7-8), whereas the evidence that Jesus believed that same-sex intimacy is OK is non-existent.

In light of Jesus' teaching on sex, Jesus' followers ask whether it's better to avoid sex and marriage entirely. (Matthew 19:10) Here is where Jesus endorses only one alternative to loving, monogamous, heterosexual marriage: contented, committed celibacy. In Matthew 19:11, Jesus seems to be as excited about celibacy as Paul was (1 Corinthians 7:8-9). Jesus says that celibacy is not for everyone, but anyone who can accept this as a lifestyle, let them do so. Jesus is the ultimate proof that we don't have to have sex or be married to be healthy, whole, or complete.

(We'll say more in chapter 7 about how we know that Jesus was not married. The evidence is slim, but it is sufficient to conclude that Jesus practiced what he preached on celibacy. Celibacy partially fits the criterion of dissimilarity; marriage was the overwhelming Jewish norm, and it is hard to explain celibacy among Christians in a sex-charged Roman world if Jesus did not strongly endorse it.)

## Jesus' Sky High Ethic

One item of historical bedrock in Jesus' teaching is unlimited forgiveness of wrongs done to us. This teaching is unparalleled anywhere in Judaism or paganism. And we find that teaching in multiple independent sound bites: Matthew 6:12 (echoing "forgive us our debts" in the Lord's Prayer just before these verses), Matthew 18:21-22 (= Luke 17:4 – forgiving seventy times seven times), Matthew 18:23-35 (the Parable of the Unforgiving Servant), Mark 11:25, and Luke 6:37. Added to this teaching is Jesus' command to love our enemies (Matthew 5:43-47 = Luke 6:27-28, 32-36), a teaching that likewise fits the criterion of dissimilarity: only one Stoic philosopher ever came close to this teaching (Epictetus, *Discourses* 3.22.53-54: the Cynic, "while he is flogged, must love those who flog him").

If I were inventing my own Jesus, I would not have included this part of the historical Jesus. Forgiveness and love of enemies are definitely where Jesus pushes me out of my comfort zone. I know he's right, and I only hurt myself if I fail to do what he says. But I can't avoid this section of historical bedrock, even though it sounds perilously close to making our standing with God conditional on whether we have forgiven everyone who has ever wronged us.

Love is a hard-to-miss part of the teaching of the historical Jesus. But love is not as common in Jesus' teaching as some people imagine. The noun *agapē* is only used twice in any of the Synoptic Gospels, and seven times in John. The verb form *agapaō* is easier to find: twenty times in the Synoptic Gospels and twenty-seven times in John. But Jesus talks much more about our need to love God than about God's love for us.

One way where Jesus stands out from the crowd is that Jesus was the only teacher in his day to identify the commands to love God and love neighbor as the two greatest commands on which all the rest of God's law depends. (Matthew 22:37-40, Mark 12:28-34) In Luke 10:25-28, Jesus uses these two love commands as a summary of what one must do to have eternal life, and then he uses his Parable of the Good Samaritan to define love of neighbor to include even the despised Samaritan. (Incidentally, except for John's account of the woman at the well, Luke is the only Gospel that pays attention to the Samaritans.)

While Jesus talks about love more in John than in the other three Gospels, in John, Jesus concentrates entirely on love for "one another" (15:17) with no mention of love for enemies. Yes, Jesus sets the bar sky-high here: "Love one another, as I have loved you." (John 13:34 = 15:12) "Greater love has no one than this: that a person lay down their life for their friends." (John 15:13*) But in the Sermon on the Mount (see above), Jesus says that a love that only loves those who love us is hardly worthy of the name.

---

in my blog post "What Did Jesus Say About Homosexuality?" at https://www.patheos.com/blogs/tomhobson/category/biblical-word-studies/, accessed 7/9/2019.

But the historical Jesus talked not just about love, but also about future judgment. While John Dominic Crossan claims that Jesus only cared about the here and now, the facts prove that the historical Jesus cared passionately about the future. Jesus warns his listeners about hell twelve times, including once by the name *Hadēs* (Luke 16:23, in the parable of the Rich Man and Lazarus), and eleven times by the name *Gehenna,* the standard Jewish name for hell, named for a 24/7 pile of burning garbage outside Jerusalem. Jesus also clearly warns his listeners about the destruction of Jerusalem that will soon come to pass (Matthew 24 = Mark 13 = Luke 21). He warns his followers to flee without delay when they see the Temple defiled, which took place in 68 AD. The fact that the early church crosses the Jordan at this time to escape the coming tribulation would seem to confirm that Jesus really did utter this warning in advance.

Jesus' unique teaching on servanthood can be found in multiple independent witnesses: Mark 9:35 and 10:35-45 (= Matthew 20:20-28), Matthew 23:11-12, Luke 22:24-27, and John 13:1-17. Luke gives us the closest connection to John, both of them reporting what Jesus said about servanthood at the Last Supper, although in John, Jesus gives a dramatic demonstration of his teaching in action when he washes his followers' feet.

In Mark 10, the disciples obviously don't grasp what it means to sit next to Jesus! They want to share his glory, but not the pain he will have to endure. (Matthew notes that it was Mrs. Zabdai/Zebedee who instigated this power grab. If she looks too pushy, remember that she stays with Jesus all the way to the cross.) William Lane comments that "selfish ambition and rivalry were the raw material from which Jesus had to fashion the leadership for the incipient Church… In their struggle for rank and precedence, and the desire to exercise authority for their own advantage, the disciples were actually imitating those whom they undoubtedly despised"[11] James Dunn concurs: "That Jesus' talk of the kingdom should have given rise to such ambition among his intimates is entirely credible, as also that the communities should cherish the memory of Jesus' rebuke as a stark reminder of where their own priorities should lie… the core memory is of Jesus depicting his role in servant terms and commending it as an example to his close circle."[12]

Jesus uses the verbs *katakurieuō* ("exercise dominion" or "lord it over") and *katexousiazō* ("domineer" or "pull rank") to describe the Gentile approach to power (the Jewish approach was not much different). Jesus declares, "It shall not be so among you." (Matthew 20:26) In his teaching on this occasion, Jesus turns King of the Hill upside down. The criteria of multiple witnesses, embarrassment (the disciples don't look good here), and dissimilarity all indicate that this teaching is another piece of undeniable historical bedrock in the life of Jesus.

Jesus gives us an ethic that is sky high. He preaches love of enemies, and practices what he preached on the cross. He tells his followers, "Unless your righteousness exceeds that of the scribes and Pharisees, you shall by no means enter the kingdom of heaven." (Matthew 5:20) Jesus goes so far as to say, "Be ye therefore perfect [*teleios,* complete or consistent], even as your Father who is in heaven is perfect." (Matthew 5:48, KJV) Even the early church tries to soften such teaching, as we see in the *Didachē* (95 AD), the earliest Christian book from outside the Bible, where we read, "For if you are able to bear all the yoke of the Lord, you shall be perfect, but if you are not able, do whatever you can." (*Didachē* 6:2) If we think we can earn our way to God, the historical Jesus demands perfection.

All in all, the historical Jesus is an extremely challenging character. In chapter 4, we will see more about his most far-reaching claims about himself, and the evidence that Jesus was who he claimed to be. But before we go there, we first want to take a look at parts of the Jesus tradition for which the evidence is slim, but which we take on faith because we trust the Bible. We'll also look at reports about Jesus from outside the Bible which may or may not pass historical scrutiny, and see whether or not they add to the picture we find in the canonical Bible.

---

[11] William L. Lane, *The Gospel of Mark* (NICNT; Grand Rapids: Eerdmans, 1974), 382.

[12] James D. G. Dunn, *Jesus Remembered* (Grand Rapids: Eerdmans, 2003), 560.

# CHAPTER 3

# UNCERTAINTIES IN THE LIFE OF JESUS

As I explained in chapter 1, many passages in the Gospels are backed up with evidence that meets the historical scholar's "criteria of authenticity" so well that you don't have to believe the Bible to say that they are solid fact. There are other passages, however, that have less grounds for support. These are parts that believers are required to take on faith, based on how many times the Gospels have proven to be reliable elsewhere. We'll take a look at a few of these passages in this chapter.

In addition, there are other accounts of Jesus' words and actions outside the Bible that appeal for our acceptance. How do we decide what merit to grant to them? Here is where the criteria of authenticity become particularly helpful, particularly the criterion of coherence, where we ask, "Does this testimony about Jesus fit with what we confidently know from elsewhere?" We'll take a look at a number of these as well. While we might conclude that some of these claims might be true, we will want to consider whether they add any important data to the picture of Jesus that God has already preserved for us in the canonical Gospels. At the same time, this study may also help confirm for us that early followers of Jesus had good reason to reject many such passages (or in some cases entire books) as inauthentic.

## Historical Gems We Almost Lost

Possibly the best example of an anecdote that hangs by a thread (from an historian's point of view) is where Luke quotes Jesus saying at the Last Supper that from now on, whoever does not have a sword should sell their garment and buy one. (Luke 22:36) What? Where did this come from? One could see how this saying of Jesus could be useful to the ancient counterparts of today's gun advocates. But how do we know that Jesus really said this?

How does this saying fit the criteria of authenticity? We find it only in Luke (no multiple sources), and when we apply the criterion of coherence, it appears to contradict the rest of what we know about Jesus, who says in Matthew 5:39*, "Do not resist one who evil." Also, later that same night, when he is being arrested, Jesus orders Peter, "Put your sword back into its place, for all who take the sword shall perish by the sword." (Matthew 26:52*) (Notice that, according to Luke, the disciples already happen to have two swords in their possession; what did they need them for?)

Could the early church have invented this saying? The early church never defended itself with the sword from Roman persecution; they followed Jesus' teaching of non-violence. However, Jesus' advice may have been intended, not for the purpose of resisting government persecution, but for protection from the lawless zealots later known as the Sicarii (described in Josephus, *Antiquities* 20:160-165) who threatened to kill anyone who cooperated with Roman rule.

So here we have a word from Jesus only found in one source, that appears to conflict with the overall picture of Jesus we get from elsewhere, while it does fit the criterion of dissimilarity from the early church (it is difficult to say how it fits with Judaism). One can argue that the saying also fits the criterion of embarrassment: why would it have been preserved, unless the facts demanded it? The criterion of embarrassment would say that no one records material that goes against what they would prefer to say, unless they find it absolutely necessary to do so.

I accept this advice to buy a sword as a genuine saying of Jesus. But we need to understand the historical grounds on which some may question the passage, and the historical arguments one can make in defense of its authenticity. These arguments become particularly helpful in assessing sayings and reports about Jesus from outside the canonical Bible.

Jesus' words as he is being nailed to the cross, "Father, forgive them, for they know not what they do," are only found in Luke 23:34a (KJV), and even there, they are missing from a large portion of the earliest manuscripts. They are missing from our oldest manuscript of Luke, P[75] (200's AD). They are missing from Codex Vaticanus (300's AD), and from the original text of Codex Bezae (they are added into the margin by a later scribe). They are also missing from two of the oldest Latin manuscripts (it[a] and it[d]), from the earliest Syriac version, and from most Coptic manuscripts. However, they can be found in the earliest text of Codex Sinaiticus (300's AD), in the vast majority of Latin manuscripts, in manuscript 33 (a late copy of a very early Greek manuscript), and in the majority of Greek copies mass-produced after the fourth century AD, plus they are quoted by Hippolytus, Justin Martyr, and Irenaeus in the second century AD, which is evidence that early writers knew this passage.

In cases like this, we must weigh the evidence rather than count the manuscripts. The fact that these words of Jesus were included in the Majority Text on which the King James Version is based proves nothing; 100 copies can be based on a late and unreliable original.

We must also ask why copyists might have added or tried to remove these words. It is probable that some in the early church rejected this saying due to their own animosity toward Jesus' killers. It is rare for words in an early Bible manuscript to be deleted by a copyist; usually, the tendency is to add words. But in this particular case, we can see why strong conviction could have led some copyists to leave this saying out as they recopied this text.

Despite the rage against Jesus' killers found in early sources, we find solid manuscript evidence that Stephen uttered a similar prayer for his killers (Acts 7:60, a verse recorded by Luke). Also, the second century AD Christian writer Hegesippus reports that James the brother of Jesus prays virtually the same words as he is executed in 62 AD.[1] Stephen and James may be echoing Jesus, which strengthens the case for Luke 23:34a.

Instead of saying "God will punish you!", like the seven Jewish brothers who are martyred by the evil Greek king Antiochus IV in 2 Maccabees 7:1-38, or Polycarp when he is about to be burned at the stake by the Romans for refusing to worship Caesar, Jesus asks God to forgive. Here from the cross is love of enemies on steroids! Renowned Jesus scholar Raymond Brown gives a strong defense of the passage's authenticity.[2]

Imagine how much we would lose from our picture of Jesus if these two passages had not been preserved! God knew that we would need them to know the whole story on Jesus. If they had not been in our Bible, and we found them in some papyrus scraps in an Egyptian garbage dump, we would want to add them into our Bibles.

The same is true of the passage where Jesus forgives the woman caught in adultery (John 7:53-8:11). The

---

[1] Quoted by Eusebius, *Ecclesiastical History* 2.23.16 (mid 300's AD).

[2] Raymond Brown, *The Death of the Messiah* (New York: Doubleday, 1994), 975-981.

manuscript evidence indicates that this passage was not an original part of the Gospel of John. It is missing from our two oldest manuscripts of John, P[66] and P[75]. It is missing from Codex Sinaiticus, Codex Vaticanus, and at least six major Greek manuscripts (plus A and C, which lack the pages where John 8 is found). These verses are missing from four Old Latin manuscripts (it[a], it[f], it[l], and it[q]), as well as from the early Syriac version and half of our Coptic manuscripts. No Greek commentary on John mentions the passage until 1100 AD, and even copies that contain this passage are marked by asterisks indicating doubt about the text's originality. The earliest Greek text where we find this story is Codex Bezae (400's AD), along with four major Greek manuscripts, the rest of our Latin manuscripts (including the Vulgate), half of our Coptic manuscripts, and the large number of Greek texts in the Majority Text on which the King James Version is based.

While the textual evidence indicates that this passage was not part of John's original, what we read here fits all of the historical criteria of authenticity except multiple independent witnesses. It fits the criterion of embarrassment: it makes Jesus look scandalously permissive. It fits the criterion of dissimilarity from Judaism and the early church, neither of whom are known for such a degree of mercy. It also fits the criterion of coherence: Jesus is well known for his kindness to notorious sinners, of which this would be the most amazing example.

We must also ask the diagnostic questions as to why such a passage would be deleted if it was original, or why it would be added if it was not original; the trend always leans toward addition. One clue that this passage was not original is that even in copies where we do find it, it is not always in the same location. Most copies put it after John 7:52, but some put it at the end of John, or even after Luke 21:38 (!). This seems to show that it was a persistent piece of early oral tradition looking for a place in Scripture.

I am convinced that John 7:53-8:11 is the best example of a floating piece of historical tradition about Jesus that really and truly happened, which deserves to be added to our canonical Bible. Think how much we lose without this scene from the life of Jesus! God made sure that it would find its place in our Bible.

## Unwritten Sayings of Jesus: Lower Quality Stones, and Fakes

In cases like these three examples, we choose to trust the Gospels even when the evidence is not as strong as we find in other passages. But what about reports about unwritten sayings of Jesus? And what about whole Gospels that never made the final publication cut, such as the Gospel of the Hebrews, the Gospel of the Nazarenes, the Gospel of the Egyptians, and the famous Gospel of Thomas?

Not every word of Jesus made it into the canonical Gospels. Imagine: if Luke hadn't given us Acts 20:35, we would have lost those famous words: "It is more blessed to give than to receive." There are more words of Jesus in the New Testament, but they are words he spoke from heaven, such as 2 Corinthians 12:9* ("My power is made perfect in weakness") and the many words he speaks in the book of Revelation. It is important that we distinguish between Jesus' earthly words, and his words from heaven. It is his earthly words that we must use as a check on claims that he has spoken from heaven.

Using the criterion of multiple independent sources to help narrow down the field, let's begin with the unwritten sayings of Jesus that are the most quoted by the early church. The following strange saying is quoted three times: "When you make the two one, and when you make the inside like the outside and the outside like the inside, and the above like the below, and when you make the male and the female one and the same, so that the male not be male nor the female female…, then you will enter the kingdom of God." (Gospel of Thomas #22, 2 Clement 12:2, Clement of Alexandria *Stromata* 3.13.92) Although the quote is widely known, these words appear to be late and Gnostic rather than the voice of Jesus. A similar saying is also quoted three times: "His disciples say unto him,

When will you be manifest unto us and when shall we see you? He says: When you have put off your raiment and are not ashamed." (Papyrus Oxyrhynchus 655, Gospel of Thomas 37, Gospel According to the Egyptians)

The Gospel of Thomas (dated around 150 AD) is a mildly Gnostic document, a viewpoint shown in supposed sayings of Jesus such as "Split a piece of wood, and I am there. Lift up the stone, and you will find me there." (Saying #77) Thomas does contain two favorites of mine that I would love to believe are genuine words of Jesus. One is Saying #102: "Jesus said, Woe to the Pharisees, for they are like a dog sleeping in the manger of oxen, for neither does he eat nor does he let the oxen eat." The dog in the manger image is found in Aesop's fables and in Lucian, both from the second century AD, so it is difficult to say if Jesus coined it. My other favorite is Saying #47: "It is impossible for a man to mount two horses or to stretch two bows." Also humorous is Saying #53: "His disciples said to him, Is circumcision beneficial or not? He said to them, If it were beneficial, their father would beget them already circumcised from their mother." If this were a genuine saying of Jesus, it would have been a slam-dunk answer to the circumcision debate in Acts 15.

Origen, Jerome, Epiphanius, and others quote Jesus saying, "Be ye approved money-changers." Clement of Alexandria adds, "because they reject much, but keep the good." (*Stromata* 1.28.177) Joachim Jeremias explains: an expert moneychanger can tell the difference between genuine and fake coins.[3] If he is correct, Jesus is urging followers to know how to spot counterfeit prophets and teachings. Because this meets the criteria of multiple independent sources and coherence (it resonates with what we know Jesus taught), it is probably historical, although one wonders why it did not get quoted in any of the canonical Gospels.

Epiphanius also gives us a line from the Gospel of the Ebionites, written for a Jewish branch of the church: "I came to destroy the sacrifices, and if ye will not cease from sacrificing, the wrath of God will not cease from you." While Jesus did come to make sacrifice no longer necessary (Hebrews 10:1-18), wouldn't there have been Jewish pushback if Jesus had taught this during his earthly ministry?

Around 400 AD, Jerome gives us four quotes from the Gospel According to the Hebrews. In chapter 2 of this book, we have the quote where Jesus wants to know why he should be baptized by John. Another is a line quoted three times by Jerome and twice by Origen: "Even now my mother the Holy Spirit has seized me by one of my hairs, and has brought me to the great mountain Tabor." A third quote is guaranteed to meet the criterion of dissimilarity from today's Church: "Never be joyful, except when you look upon your brother in love."

Jerome's final quote from the Gospel According to the Hebrews is somebody's attempt to give us a sound bite from Jesus' resurrection appearance to James: "Now the Lord, when he had given the linen cloth to the servant of the priest, went to James and appeared to him (for James had sworn that he would not eat bread from that hour when he had drunk the Lord's cup until he should see him risen again from among them that sleep)...he took bread and blessed and broke and gave it to James the Just and said to him: My brother, eat your bread, for the Son of Man is risen from among them that sleep." I find it extremely doubtful that James believed that Jesus would rise, certainly not enough that he would fast until Jesus rose.

Papias (100 AD), as quoted by Irenaeus in 180 AD, gives us Jesus' reported description of the future golden age: "The days are coming when vines will come forth...and in every cluster will be ten thousand grapes, and every grape, when pressed, will yield twenty-five measures of wine... So too a grain of wheat will produce ten thousand heads...and every grain will yield ten pounds of pure, exceptionally fine flour... And all the animals who eat this food drawn from the earth will come to be at peace and harmony with one another, yielding in complete submission to humans." This quote is intriguing, because it is very early, but it is also found as a description of the age of

---

[3] Joachim Jeremias, *Unknown Sayings of Jesus* (Eugene: Wipf and Stock, reprint of 1963 edition), 90.

the Messiah's coming in a Jewish apocalypse, 2 Baruch 29. Does Jesus talk about the future in such earthly terms in his teachings in our canonical Gospels?

The Talmud preserves one more sound bite that I suspect may truly be from Jesus. A Galilean Christian named James asks Rabbi Eliezer ben Hyrcanus whether "the hire of a harlot" can be used to build a latrine for the high priest, contrary to Deuteronomy 23:18. James then says, "Thus did Jeshu of Nazareth teach me: 'From the hire of a harlot was it gathered, and to the hire of a harlot shall it return.' (Micah 1:7) From filth it came, and to filth shall it return again." ('Abodah Zarah 16b 17a) To me, I hear the same brilliance of a Torah teacher here that I see in the Jesus of the Gospels. But even if Jesus said this, of what use is this saying to followers of Jesus? Here we can see how and why some words that may have been truly spoken by Jesus were not found necessary to be included in the Gospels.

In addition, there are two sizeable Gospel fragments that have been unearthed in Egypt. One is Papyrus Oxyrhynchus 840,[4] where Jesus rebukes a priest in the Temple. The priest asks, Who gave you permission to come in here without bathing? Jesus answers that he has bathed in the pool of David and has put on clean clothes, but then Jesus accuses the priest of bathing himself in water used by dogs, swine, and prostitutes.

The other text is known as the Egerton Gospel Fragment, which reads like a mixture of echoes from John and the other Gospels.[5] Jesus repeats the words of John 5:39 and 5:45, to which the lawyers answer, "We know well that God spoke to Moses, but you, we don't know where you come from." They advise that Jesus be stoned, but Jesus slips away through the midst of them. Jesus then heals a leper who says he caught leprosy from other lepers at an inn. Another group asks him, "Master Jesus, we know that you come from God, for the things you do testify above all the prophets. Tell us therefore: Is it lawful to render unto kings that which pertains to their rule?" Jesus answers, "Why call me Master with your mouth, when you don't hear what I say?" He then proceeds to quote the line from Isaiah 29:13, "This people honors me with their lips, but their heart is far from me." (Matthew 15:8*)

The Gospel of Peter (around 100 AD?) merits some consideration historically. All we possess are the parts about Jesus' burial and resurrection. While this text presents the strange picture of a risen Jesus so tall that he stomps out of his tomb with his head higher than the heavens, it gives details that may be true, such as the name Petronius for the centurion who guarded Jesus' tomb. However, the Gospel of Peter is otherwise heavily dependent on Matthew.

When we apply the criteria of authenticity to reported unwritten sayings of Jesus outside the Gospels, a few sayings might appear to be historical, but they add little to what we already know about Jesus, while others do not fit what we know about the historical Jesus at all. And when we see the legends that our present Gospels leave out, our confidence in what the Gospels do tell us about Jesus is strengthened. For instance, the Infancy Gospel of Thomas pictures Jesus as an unholy terror who pronounces fatal curses on children and adults who displease him, and who makes clay pigeons and brings them to life. This is not the Jesus we know from our canonical Gospels; he flunks the criterion of coherence. We need not wonder why such books were left out of our Bible. None of these parts that were left out qualify as "plain and precious."

While there are some parts of our canonical Gospels that require faith beyond what history can establish, there is a huge amount that we can know about the historical Jesus even if we have no commitment to Biblical authority. Now it's time to apply the criteria of authenticity to the claims of the Gospels that Jesus was far more than a man. Are these claims sufficiently sound to command faith?

---

[4] Text in Wilhelm Schneemelcher, ed., *New Testament Apocrypha* (Philadelphia: Westminster, 1963), 1: 94-95.

[5] Text in H. Idris Bell and T.C. Skeat, eds., *Fragments of an Unknown Gospel* (London: British Museum, 1935), 28.

CHAPTER 4

# EXAMINING THE WILDEST CLAIMS ABOUT JESUS

So far, we've uncovered a lot of historical bedrock in the life of Jesus, including the undeniable testimony that Jesus performed literal miracles. We've also examined points where the evidence for his deeds and words is not so strong, and sometimes must be taken on faith. We've also examined claims about Jesus' life that simply do not pass historical scrutiny nor merit our trust. Having done so, we turn to the most far reaching and most important claims about his life: his miraculous conception, his claims to be far more than a man, and his resurrection.

## Jesus' Miraculous Conception

The Virgin Conception of Jesus is a truly astounding claim. While laboratory evidence for this claim is not obtainable, this claim is supported by strong logical evidence.

Neither Mark nor Paul makes any explicit reference to the Virgin Birth, although Mark 6:3 records that when Jesus comes back to Nazareth, the people refer to him as "the son of Mary." Naming only a child's mother usually happened in Biblical times only when the father was unknown, making this a possible slur on Jesus' parentage.

The account of the Virgin Birth seems to first appear in the time when Matthew and Luke publish their Gospels, i.e. no earlier than the early 60's AD. Why the apparent silence until this date? It's easy to understand how such a piece of sensitive, hard-to-explain information was kept private within Mary and Joseph's family until after the death of Mary, who was probably in her late 70's by 60 AD. The two conception narratives are independent, and reflect a tradition going back even earlier than their present form.

Why would the early church have invented a claim that was so easily misunderstood, if not downright embarrassing? Larry Hurtado observes, "To claim a miraculous conception with no identifiable father does not appear terribly wise if early Christians simply wanted to refute successfully the slur that Jesus was illegitimate."[1] The church never would have made such a claim if they were not compelled to by the facts. Jesus was not the natural child of Joseph and Mary, and he was not anyone else's child, either. These facts were not common knowledge, but when it was appropriate to do so, God's people ended up putting them in writing.

The church may have done so because of speculation outside the church. Ethelbert Stauffer writes that according to the rabbis of Jesus' day, "If a man is suspected of apostasy, the circumstances of his birth are to be investigated. For the *mamser* [illegitimate child]…is inclined toward rebellion and blasphemy… As long as a *mamser* leads a life

---

[1] Hurtado, *Lord Jesus Christ*, 322.

pleasing to God, nothing insulting shall be said about his birth… If the *mamser* becomes an apostate, his illegitimate birth shall be spoken of publicly and unsparingly."[2] (Stauffer gives all the references.)

So Stauffer thinks the people of Nazareth kept quiet about their suspicions until Jesus' teachings start getting questioned. Later on, Celsus the pagan charged that Jesus was fathered by a Roman soldier named Panthera, although Meier has solidly argued that these particular rumors are late and not from Palestine.[3] Meier places the date of the rumor between the time of Justin Martyr (140 AD?) and Celsus (178 AD). In Justin's debate with Trypho the Jew about the Virgin Birth, Trypho makes no mention of this rumor.

Why didn't the church counter that Jesus was merely born of Joseph and Mary? If Matthew is to be trusted, Joseph knew otherwise. The "criterion of embarrassment" applies here: Matthew and Luke are compelled to report this fact about Jesus' birth because the facts leave them no alternative.

It has been alleged that the idea of the Virgin Birth is just borrowed from pagan mythology. But as J. Gresham Machen proved in his book *The Virgin Birth of Christ*, the New Testament claims are far different from those of pagan mythology. All of the pagan myths cited in this regard involve physical sex, and some involved married women. As Cambridge scholar C. E. B. Cranfield says, "The church may well have sensed the danger that the Virgin Birth, if proclaimed in the Gentile world, would be misunderstood along the lines of the pagan myths, as being like the birth of a Perseus or a Heracles, or as a mere flattering fancy like the stories of the births of Plato, Alexander, [or] Augustus."[4]

Is this simply a matter of a prescientific point of view held by gullible people? No, people in the first century AD were far from ignorant about nature. There would have been no big deal if births like this happen all the time. People at this time understood that a birth like this breaks the laws of nature. And yet, science knows that virgin births do happen all the time in the animal world. It's called parthenogenesis (literally "virgin-generation"). The only catch is that it always produces a female offspring. (Who put the Y-chromosome in this one?)

The Virgin Birth was not a part of the church's evangelism to the outside world. It was not used to present Jesus in competition to pagan heroes. It was inside information for believers. It only takes on importance in the early second century, when Ignatius cites Jesus' birth as proof that Jesus was truly human and not a ghost.

Did Jesus have to be born by a miraculous birth to be the sinless Son of God? No, but it only makes sense that the Second Adam would be brought into existence by a brand new act of creation. We cannot prove the Virgin Birth in a test tube, but neither can it be disproved, and the unlikelihood of its being invented or volunteered by followers of Jesus is a significant argument in favor of its historicity, even if history is hesitant to speak of miracles.

Cranfield summarizes well: "It is, surely, extremely difficult, on the assumption that the Virgin Birth is not historical, to explain at all convincingly how the early church came during the first century to affirm it, in spite of the fact that there was no expectation that the Messiah would be virgin-born, in spite of the certainty that such an affirmation would be met by incredulity and ridicule among Jews…, and in spite of the obvious danger that among Gentiles the doctrine would be misunderstood along the lines of pagan mythology."[5]

---

[2] Ethelbert Stauffer, *Jesus and His Story* (New York: Alfred A. Knopf, 1960), 207.

[3] Meier, *Marginal Jew*, 2:223-25.

[4] C. E. B. Cranfield, *On Romans and Other New Testament Essays* (Edinburgh: T and T Clark, 2001), 162.

[5] Cranfield, *Romans*, 163.

## Jesus' Claims to Be God

Likewise, Jesus' claims to be divine are readily shown to be, not the later inventions of the early church,[6] but an unavoidable fact that played a major role in his trial and crucifixion. Jesus goes around talking and acting like he is God.

It all starts slowly and subtly. Jesus raises eyebrows when he tells the paralyzed man, "Your sins are forgiven you," and onlookers accuse him of blasphemy, objecting, "Who can forgive sins but God alone?", a triply attested piece of historical bedrock (Matthew 9:2-3, Mark 2:5-7, Luke 5:20-21). Also undoubtedly historical is his claim to be "Lord of the Sabbath," the one who has the authority to speak for God on the subject (Matthew 12:8, Mark 2:28, Luke 6:5). Likewise, we are on historical bedrock when Jesus' stilling of the storm leads his followers to ask, "Who then is this, that even wind and sea obey him?" (Matthew 8:27*, Mark 4:41*, similarly Luke 8:25)

The climactic scene where Jesus' followers finally begin to come to terms with who he is happens at Caesarea Philippi, at the source of the Jordan River. Here the ancient Canaanites had built a shrine called Baal-Gad, "The Lord of Fortune." Hundreds of years later, the Greeks had built a temple to Pan, the god of nature. And recently, Herod's brother Philip had built a temple here for the worship of Augustus Caesar, and had named the nearby town after Caesar ("Caesarea of Philip").

Here in the woods at the source of the Jordan, surrounded by pagan shrines, Jesus asks, "Who do people say that I am?" The answers he gets back prove how wrong polls can be. Every answer they give is wrong. Out of all those surveyed in this poll, only one guy gets anywhere near the right answer. Simon Peter answers, "You are the Messiah, the Son of the living God." (Matthew 16:16*) Here, surrounded by the shrines of other gods (the Baal of Fortune, the Greek god of nature, the temple of Caesar), Jesus lays his identity on the line. He claims to be both the Jewish Messiah, and the Son of the living God. Jesus claims to stand taller than any competing claim on the Jewish or Gentile market.

Peter's answer to the ultimate poll question becomes the rock on which we stand. Like the Jordan River that flows downhill from here, twenty-five miles and 1700 feet in elevation downward to the Sea of Galilee, the question "Who is Jesus Christ?" is a watershed dividing line. Where our faith goes is determined by the answer we give here.

Is Jesus accepting or rejecting Peter's declaration? Blomberg writes that although "Peter seems to grasp some of Jesus' unique relationship with God, he is still not prepared for a suffering Messiah who refuses to overthrow Rome or promote Jewish nationalism. That is why Jesus must silence him for the time being."[7] So contrary to those who claim that Jesus never claims to be Messiah or Son of God (if "Son of God" is not an anachronism in the mouth of Peter), Jesus accepts Peter's words, but not what he thinks they mean.

But how do we know that this scene really and truly happened? How do we know it wasn't made up? The first argument in favor of its authenticity is, Why would they have chosen this unexpected place, and not somewhere else? It has been argued that Mark deliberately puts the scene here to contrast Jesus with pagan gods and the emperor cult. It has been further argued that because Jesus never attacks foreign religions, therefore this scene was made up by Mark, although one could argue instead that here is evidence that Jesus did so. But because Jesus is moving away from Jerusalem at this point, and because the next scene is on a high mountain (probably Mount Hermon), it is logical to find him somewhere in this area. He's only been this far north recently, when he heals the Canaanite woman's daughter, so this memory is probably authentic.

---

[6] One of the strongest cases that the Deity of Christ was not a late invention but goes back to the very earliest church is made by Hurtado, *Lord Jesus Christ*, 19-216.

[7] Blomberg, *Jesus*, 323.

Another argument for the authenticity of this passage is the embarrassing picture it gives us of Peter, and if Mark is writing down what Peter tells him, so much the more convincing. As John Meier puts it, "the early church would hardly have gone out of its way to create material that only embarrassed its creator or weakened its position in arguments with opponents."[8] The kicker is the line, "Get behind me, Satan!"

(Note also that there is an echo of Peter's confession in John 6:68-69, where the crowds are starting to turn away from Jesus. There are huge differences, but that may mean we have independent witnesses. Or it may mean that these were two different incidents, although which one came first is not clear.)

Peter's confession also passes the coherence test. If Jesus ever affirmed that he was the Messiah, someone from among his closest followers must have raised the issue.

It is commonly objected that the mention of a church and Peter's leadership of it are anachronisms that were invented later. (*Ekklēsia*, "church," only gets used two places in any of the four Gospels.) But by picking twelve apostles (another piece of historical bedrock), surely Jesus had plans to create a community of followers. And how else would Peter have ended up leading that community, without a self-fulfilling prophecy like this one?

Peter's confession that Jesus is the unique Son of God is followed by his Transfiguration on nearby snow-capped Mount Hermon, where Jesus' face and clothes begin shining brighter than the sun, and Jesus' inner circle hears the words from heaven, "This is my beloved Son." This scene is attested, not only in Matthew 17:1-5, Mark 9:2-7, and Luke 9:28-35, but also in 2 Peter 1:16-18, where Peter reaches back to his memory of that day as his evidence that he was an eyewitness of Jesus' divine glory, and that he was not inventing "cleverly devised myths."

Until the sergeant utters his famous confession "Truly this man was the Son of God" at the cross (Mark 15:39), "Son of God" almost always appears only in the words of Satan or demons, or God. Exceptions include the disciples in Matthew 14:33 after Jesus walks on the water, Nathaniel in John 1:49, and Martha just before Jesus raises Lazarus in John 11:27. We hear the words "Holy One of God" during Jesus' first case of exorcism in the Capernaum synagogue (Mark 1:24, Luke 4:34), and "Son of God" in Jesus' triply-attested super-exorcism of the Gerasene demoniac (Matthew 8:29, Mark 5:7, Luke 8:28).

Jesus can speak of a father-son relationship with God, but his words can be understood in more than one way. Dunn observes that Jesus refers to God as Father only three or four times in Mark and Q, while he does so in Matthew more than thirty times, and 100 times in John.[9]

Only when Jesus bluntly answers "I am" to the question at his trial, "Are you the Messiah, the Son of the Blessed One?" (Mark 14:61-62*), can we say for sure what Jesus is claiming for himself in the Synoptic Gospels. In John, however, Jesus says, "Before Abraham was, I am" (8:58), "I and the Father are one" (10:30*), and "Whoever has seen me has seen the Father" (14:8*). How many of these can be dismissed, and how many of them pass the rigorous tests of incontestable authenticity? Certainly they pass the test of rejection: such claims definitely help explain why Jesus was crucified.

But even in the supposedly earliest layer of tradition, in Q (the hypothetical book of sayings quoted by both Matthew and Luke), we find a Jesus who demands decision. Jesus is the polarizing issue. "Whoever does not gather with me, scatters." (Matthew 12:30* = Luke 11:23) Q constantly forces us to decide for or against Jesus. See Matthew 10:32-42* (= Luke 12:51-53 + 14:25-33): "Whoever denies me before humans, I also will deny before my Father in heaven… Whoever loves father or mother more than me is not worthy of me… Whoever welcomes you welcomes me, and whoever welcomes me welcomes the One who sent me." Also, in Matthew 11:25-30* (partial parallel in

---

[8]  Meier, *Marginal Jew*, 1:168.

[9]  Dunn, *Jesus Remembered*, 708.

Luke 10:21-22), Jesus speaks in language like John: "No one knows the Father but the Son." His audience may not have been thinking "Son of God," but they remembered this line, and later it made much more sense.

Jesus teaches that he will be the Judge on the final Day of Judgment (Matthew 25:31-46). He promises to hear and answer the prayers of his disciples (John 14:13-14). And he accepts worship that belongs to God alone (Matthew 14:33, John 20:28).

The historical Jesus acted and talked like he was God. If Joseph Smith had spoken and behaved this way, we would be uncomfortable, and we would have much more reason to understand why he was killed. Jesus claims devotion that belongs to God alone.

## Jesus' Resurrection: The Bedrock for All Historical Bedrock

The evidence for Jesus' resurrection proves to be stronger than for any other key event from ancient times. Without Jesus' resurrection, we would have no reason to pay any attention to Jesus other than as an interesting historical figure. This event helps make perfect sense out of why Jesus acted and talked like he was God.

Before we have a resurrection we can prove, we first need to nail down the facts about his burial. Here, Crossan is famous for insisting that crucified criminals were denied burial, and that Jesus would have been thrown into a common grave and eaten by dogs. The Mishnah prescribes a place outside Jerusalem for the burial of executed criminals (Sanhedrin 6:7). Tacitus (*Annals* VI.29) says that under Tiberius, "people sentenced to death forfeited their property and were forbidden burial." However, archaeological evidence is well-known for a crucifixion victim whose bones were unearthed in a family tomb, with the nail still through the ankles.[10] Both Philo (*Flaccus* 83) and Josephus (*Jewish War* 4:377) narrate instances of such burial permission being granted. Special permission appears to have been given for Jesus as well.

Joseph of Arimathea is recognized to be a "very plausible historical character." He is attested in all four Gospels plus the Gospel of Peter. He is from a town very difficult to identify, with no Christian symbolism. Who would invent burial by a sympathizer among the villains, particularly a member of the Sanhedrin itself? Joseph's request took more courage than Peter showed, because here we have a non-relative whose request puts his own status with the Romans at risk. If Pilate had any doubts that Jesus was innocent, he never would have granted the body.

Joseph's unused tomb guarantees that later, those who look for his body would go to the right place, and could not confuse his body with others. (It also would have been tacky for a king to be buried in a used tomb.) The tomb would have ceased to be used after the new city wall was built in the early 40's. Some of the same women who witnessed the cross also witnessed the place where he was buried (but for some reason, we see no cooperation between the women and Joseph). One wonders why Joseph's tomb happened to be so close. Only Matthew says it was his. Did he use it temporarily, perhaps? Only John and the Gospel of Peter mention that there was a garden here (Jerusalem's Garden Gate was named after it). In 2016, the slab on which Jesus was laid was officially unearthed, underneath a slab put there by the Crusaders.[11]

The only unusual part of the story here is the seventy-five pounds of spices (a Roman pound was twelve

---

[10] Vassilios Tzaferis, "Crucifixion – The Archaeological Evidence," *Biblical Archaeology Review* 11, no. 1 (Jan/Feb 1985): 44-53.

[11] Kristin Romey, "Unsealing of Christ's Reputed Tomb Turns Up New Revelations," *National Geographic Online* (10/31/2016), online: https://news.nationalgeographic.com/2016/10/jesus-christ-tomb-burial-church-holy-sepulchre/, accessed 4/19/2019. The site described here is the Church of the Holy Sepulcher. The alternative site suggested for Jesus' burial is the Garden Tomb near Gordon's Calvary. Evidence shows that the emperor Hadrian defiled a Judeo-Christian holy site at the Holy Sepulcher church, as if to indicate that the church in 135 AD believed that this was the site of Jesus' tomb. If the Holy Sepulcher is not the right site, it would mean that within 100 years, Christians had forgotten where Jesus died and rose. I find that hard to believe!

ounces), to which the women plan to add after the Sabbath. (A similar amount of spices is burned for the funeral of Rabbi Gamaliel.) Nicodemus is also named by John as being one of those who prepared Jesus' body. Joseph and Nicodemus cannot eat the Passover unless they have servants to do the work here. Those who bring spices are not expecting resurrection. By contrast, according to Mark, Joseph only buys a linen shroud, as if it were a rush job. The Mishnah (Shabbat 23:5) states that on the Sabbath, "They may prepare all the requirements for a corpse, anoint it, and wash it, provided only that they do not move any one of the limbs." No one who is not a follower of Jesus would go to such trouble.

The request to set a guard occurs only in Matthew and in the Gospel of Peter, where Petronius is the name of the sergeant in charge. The tomb has been unguarded all Friday night, but the soldiers would have checked it before sealing the tomb. The sealing is alleged to be a Christian apologetic invention. It is curious that the other Gospels don't mention it, but if giving away the body of a supposed traitor posed a security risk (Pilate obviously doesn't think so in this case), then this move becomes highly plausible. Brown asks, "Why are apologetics and historicity incompatible?"[12] He suggests that the presence of a guard might have been unimportant until Matthew's day, when the charge starts circulating that the body was stolen. And might not Joseph himself have wanted a guard?

Not much later than this, Tiberius issues a decree found on stone in Nazareth (of all places!) promising stiff punishment for anyone caught vandalizing tombs, including those who have removed and disposed of bodies, or transferred them to other places.[13]

The resurrection appearances come from both Jerusalem and Galilee. How do we put the two together? John has the disciples in Jerusalem even eight days later when Jesus appears to Thomas; this would mean they stayed for the whole eight-day feast of Unleavened Bread. During the next thirty-two days, they evidently go back to Galilee, where Jesus appears for the Great Commission and for John's miraculous catch of fish. (The Great Commission might be where the appearance to 500 mentioned in 1 Corinthians 15:6 takes place.) Then, they are back at the Mount of Olives for the Ascension, ten days before the next Jewish festival. Luke 24 gives the impression that the eleven disciples never left Jerusalem, but in his Gospel, Luke portrays an ascension that looks much sooner than what he describes more clearly in Acts.

The empty tomb and Jesus' presence in the room Sunday night both belong together – neither of them makes sense without the other. So we start with the tomb. Unlike the Gospel of Peter, none of the canonical Gospels have coverage of Jesus leaving the tomb, although Matthew has coverage of the angel rolling the stone away, and the guards passing out. In Matthew, this angel announces to the two Mary's that Jesus has risen, after which Jesus meets them on the way back from the tomb. In Mark, there are three women (add Salome), who meet a young man in white inside the tomb. They flee and "said nothing to anyone, for they were afraid" (if Mark ends with 16:8).[14]

We don't find this story anywhere before Mark's Gospel; not in Acts, not in Paul. One reason is that women

---

[12] Brown, *Death of the Messiah*, 1310.

[13] Brown, *Death of the Messiah*, 1293.

[14] The two oldest Greek manuscripts of Mark end at 16:8. There are two additions that seem to date to the second century: verses 9-20, and a one-verse summary that begins "But they reported briefly to Peter…" Verses 9-20 are also missing from the earliest Syriac and Latin manuscripts. We must ask: if these endings were actually original, why would they be missing from the earliest manuscripts? However, if these endings were not original, why would they be added, and why are there two? The answer seems to be that Mark was never finished, and his ending seems abrupt. Mark 16:9-20 has details that are difficult to reconcile with the other Gospels. One example: 16:12-13 seems to indicate that the men on the Emmaus Road were not believed. Another example: Jesus scolding his followers for their unbelief is found nowhere else in the canonical resurrection accounts. I concur with Wright (*Resurrection*, 623-624) that Mark probably wrote a longer ending, which Matthew echoes. I am guessing that it included reassuring appearances to the women (and possibly Peter?), and some version of the Great Commission. But God evidently decided that Mark's original ending was not necessary for us to have.

were viewed as unreliable witnesses. If the disciples had invented this story, they would have used Peter and John as witnesses. Secondly, the women's account proves nothing that was not already conceded by both sides; everyone knew the tomb was empty. But the most important reason why the women and the church kept their mouths shut at first, as Frank Morison observes, is the potentially damaging weakness that it puts the women at the scene of the alleged crime at a suspiciously early hour of the morning. Would they have invented a story with such an embarrassing weakness? Now we can see why the disciples are in hiding later on that day!

In Luke, the women are the two Mary's, plus Joanna, and the "other women," and they meet two men in dazzling apparel, after which they report to the disciples, who do not believe them, although (according to some manuscripts, plus John's Gospel) Peter runs to check it out.

John has Mary Magdalene by herself, who finds the tomb empty, and reports to Peter that they have taken the Lord away (who witnesses the empty tomb). Mary then looks into the tomb and sees two angels, sitting at opposite ends of the place where Jesus' body once lay. Mary then meets Jesus outside the tomb and mistakes him for the gardener. Jesus is neither dazzling with glory here, nor is he a resuscitated corpse.

It is often objected that the inconsistencies between the accounts disprove their trustworthiness. However, Wright argues that they are "a strong point in favor of their early character. The later we imagine them being written up, the more likely it would be that inconsistencies would be ironed out."[15] Michael Licona agrees: "discrepancies among peripheral details do not necessitate wholesale invention."[16] Licona cites events from the lives of Nero and Socrates. He cites events such as the burning of Rome by Nero: "Did Nero openly send men to torch the city, as Suetonius reports, or did he do it secretly, as Dio Cassius reports, or was he not at all responsible, as Tacitus suggests is possible? Did Nero watch the city burn from the Tower of Maecenas, as Suetonius reports, or from his palace roof, as Dio reports, or was he thirty-five miles away in Antium, per Tacitus?"[17] Xenophon and Plato have very different accounts of the words of Socrates. There are two very different accounts of Hannibal crossing the Alps. No one denies that any of these are historical, yet the accounts are full of discrepancies far worse than the Easter accounts. Even events from our own lifetimes such as 9/11 and the Columbine shootings are full of details that do not match up, but we know without a doubt that they happened.

Unbiased witnesses are the hardest to find. How do you find an unbiased witness to an atomic bomb? One might ask, "You say the Gospel witnesses were all Christians. Yes, but what made them Christians?"

Secondary appearances of Jesus begin with Luke's account of the two men on the Emmaus Road (Luke 24:13-40a). Notice that they do not recognize him at first (the risen Jesus is not obvious – they're not looking for him under every rock). The men rush back to Jerusalem that night, where they hear that Jesus has appeared to Peter (we never get to hear that story). Both here and at the same scene in John 20, Jesus goes right through locked doors or walls. Here Jesus gives them proof that he is not a ghost. (See the article "The Ghost of Jesus," where the resurrection appearances are contrasted with the apparitions of dead Greco-Roman heroes.[18])

Jesus then appears to Thomas (John 20:24-29), and then to a crowd in Galilee, where some doubt (Matthew 28:16-17). Thomas can identify him by his scars. We see clearly in these texts that Jesus' resurrection is not a metaphor. It is not an experience disconnected from physical reality.

---

[15] Wright, *Resurrection*, 612.

[16] Michael R. Licona, *The Resurrection of Jesus: A New Historiographical Approach* (Downers Grove: IVP Academic, 2010), 596.

[17] Licona, *Resurrection*, 598.

[18] Deborah Thompson Prince, "The Ghost of Jesus: Luke 24 in Light of Ancient Narratives of Post-Mortem Apparitions," *Journal for the Study of the New Testament* 29, no. 3 (2007): 287-301.

The number one alternative to the truth of Jesus' resurrection is still the unauthorized removal of the body. It is the automatic conclusion to which all of the earliest persons on the scene jump. The vast majority of scholars are agreed that the eleven disciples are too dispirited and too fearful to pull off such a theft. Men who ran away from their Master and denied they ever knew him? The idea has never crossed their minds.

But what about some other joker out there? What about Joseph of Arimathea, someone who had a motive to vindicate Jesus, unbeknownst to the other disciples? Couldn't such a deceiver remove his body and burn it or feed it to the dogs? Again, most unbelieving scholars do not go there. The consensus is that in that time and culture, it was unthinkable that anyone would steal his body and trash it. What's the point in stealing a dead Messiah and claiming he's alive, while sitting on evidence to the contrary in your backyard? The only conceivable such character would be someone who had no sympathy for Jesus or his movement, but who just wanted to poke the chief priests in the eye. I cannot believe that such a person ever existed.

Because, if we look closer, we'll see that the empty tomb is not empty after all. Look at the grave clothes left behind. What robber would have taken the time and trouble to unwrap the body and arrange to leave it looking like the body had escaped? John states that Jesus was wrapped in *othnia* (bandages), and that Peter and John saw them, plus the *soudarion* (headcloth) *entetuligmenon* "wrapped up," the same verb for what Joseph of Arimathea did with the bandages to Jesus. (The Synoptic Gospels say that Joseph wrapped Jesus in a *sindōn*, a linen sheet, the same noun used for what the young man was wearing in Mark 14:51-52.)

The problem with the wrong tomb theory is that there were too many witnesses, including Joseph of Arimathea, who knew where to find his own tomb. The swoon theory was rejected even by the skeptic David Friedrich Strauss. Crucifixion was so consistently fatal that even when Josephus (*Vita* 4.75) reports having persuaded a Roman governor to have mercy and spare three crucifixion victims, two still died after they were taken down. Most modern rejecters of a bodily resurrection tend to ignore the issue of where did the body go, if anywhere, as if the issue would have been irrelevant to those on the scene, whether followers of Jesus or their opponents.

Still others are prepared to even concede that the body of Jesus actually disappeared from the tomb, but they contend that it became a "spiritual" body instead of a tangible one. Here we have some truth to contend with. Paul does contrast the physical body (*psychikon*, literally "soul-like") with the *pneumatikon* or "spiritual" body. (1 Corinthians 15:44-46) But when we examine all the evidence, we will see that physical versus spiritual is really an issue of mortality, not tangibility. It is a contrast between bodies that are subject to disease, death, and decay, and bodies that are not. Jesus is raised with the second kind of body, the prototype for our resurrected bodies (Philippians 3:20, 1 John 3:2). But it does not mean that a spiritual body is therefore non-physical, meaning that it cannot be touched. This issue is extremely important to the writer of John's Gospel and Epistles, who is trying to prove that Jesus is not a ghost, but has a body that can be touched (John 20:24-29; 1 John 1:1, 4:2).

History can never be proved measured by standards employed in a laboratory. But an examination of the evidence gives us strong reason to believe that Jesus of Nazareth was born without biological human father, performed numerous supernatural feats (as conceded even by his enemies), spoke in ways that would lead a monotheistic audience to believe that he thought he was divine, and appears to have risen alive from the tomb in which he was buried after public execution on a cross. It doesn't take faith in the Bible or any holy book to draw such conclusions.

If these conclusions are true, this Jesus is worthy of our complete confidence. All indications are that this Jesus is who he claimed to be, and that he lived a life consistent with his teachings. He appears to be uniquely qualified to lead us to the truth about God. Now, we turn our attention to Joseph Smith, to see if the facts about him confirm the claims made by him and on his behalf.

# CHAPTER 5

# WHO CAN TELL US THE TRUTH ABOUT JOSEPH?

The search for the historical Joseph will be somewhat different from the search for the historical Jesus. The criteria we will need to use most frequently are the criteria of multiple independent sources, coherence, and embarrassment. Even the criterion of rejection can come into play, wherever Joseph's acts or words help explain why he was rejected and killed.

The criterion of dissimilarity will only be needed if we find ourselves faced with a picture of Joseph that looks too much like the church that he founded. Granted, we would expect that Joseph's church would bear at least some resemblance to his teaching and example. But we can be more confident that we are on historical bedrock when we find words or acts in the life of Joseph that stand in contrast to his church, details that the later LDS church would not have invented to make him look like them.

## Evaluating the Sources

The works of the LDS Church History Department, Richard Bushman, Fawn Brodie, and Jerald and Sandra Tanner give us a variety of portraits of Joseph Smith. The recent Smith biography *Saints: The Standard of Truth* produced by the LDS Church is one place where we might apply the criterion of dissimilarity. While the book avoids the extreme of making Joseph too much like a hero larger than life, and while the book attempts to address difficulties in his life that LDS authorities have tended to avoid, it tends to err on the side of being overly sympathetic and protective toward Joseph's image.

From the other side of the spectrum comes the work of Jerald and Sandra Tanner. Their research and conclusions on Joseph may be described as meticulous, fair, but definitely from a critical perspective. They have dared to publish large amounts of primary source material that the LDS Church sought for years to avoid releasing. Yet in the early 1980's, when the Church unwittingly purchased fake documents that cast Joseph in an unflattering light, it was the Tanners who first suspected forgery. Like competent prosecutors, the Tanners make their case, and make it thoroughly. They know where to find the evidence.

In between these two perspectives are Fawn Brodie's *No Man Knows My History* and Richard Bushman's *Joseph Smith: Rough Stone Rolling*. Brodie's work was groundbreaking in that hers was the first comprehensive critical biography of Joseph ever attempted. Brodie's picture of Joseph is thoroughly human. She admires him, but she tends to inject quite a few naturalistic assumptions into her attempts to describe Joseph's thoughts and explain his actions. One wonders to what extent she might do the same with Jesus. Any reader who is seeking to know the truth about both Jesus and Joseph from a theistic perspective will utilize Brodie's work with caution.

Bushman's book is the most evenhanded study of Joseph that I can find from a sympathetic point of view. It gives the reader all the facts that both supporters and critics would want to know about Joseph to make a fully-informed decision about him. His book rivals even the works of the Tanners as a collection of hard-to-find source material. While Brodie was eventually excommunicated after writing her book, Bushman's book was highly praised when it was reviewed in the LDS-owned *Deseret News*, although his view on the historicity of Joseph's Book of Mormon seems to be that the book need not be factual to be true. Bushman is the first book toward which I would point the LDS seeker to dig deeper into the facts about Joseph than the present book is designed to do.

Now, whom do we trust among the many firsthand witnesses to the life of Joseph Smith? Which sources are the most reliable? I suggest we begin by prioritizing Joseph's own words: the three LDS canonical scriptures that come from his hand, his *History of the Church*, and his diaries, including extracts published in church magazines. Next in line are friendly witnesses to his words and actions, including church leaders and family members, with early quotes being preferable to later recollections. Last would be neutral and hostile witnesses, which must further be sorted by temporal and personal proximity to Joseph. While we may be disinclined to accept criticism of Joseph by his enemies, when an enemy makes a positive statement about Joseph, the criterion of embarrassment applies. And when claims by Joseph's enemies are backed up by friends and even by his own words, those claims deserve a second look.

Some of the sources that we use to find reliable information on Joseph are not easy to obtain and not convenient to own, but can easily be accessed online. Here are a few of the most valuable:

- Joseph Smith's *History of the Church*: https://byustudies.byu.edu/history-of-the-church
- Joseph Smith's diary: www.josephsmithpapers.org
- *Millennial Star*: Publishes much of Joseph's diary in installments, much of which was then reproduced in *History of the Church*. See https://archive.org and search for Millennial Star with volume number.
- *Times and Seasons*: http://www.centerplace.org/history/ts/default.htm
- *Journal of Discourses*: https://en.wikisource.org/wiki/Journal_of_Discourses

It is difficult to say how much to trust the word of Joseph's three early confidants, the original witnesses to the Book of Mormon. They were the first to testify that they saw the golden plates from which the book was translated. All three maintained their faith in the Book of Mormon until they died, but all three stopped following Joseph Smith. In 1838, Oliver Cowdery (the scribe who recorded Joseph's translation of the Book of Mormon) and Martin Harris were both excommunicated after both accused Joseph of lying and sexual misconduct. At the same time, David Whitmer wrote that God told him to separate himself from the Latter-day Saints, after which he joined a Book of Mormon sect called the Church of Christ, and tells us why he did so in his 1887 pamphlet *An Address to All Believers in Christ*.[1] Cowdery became a Methodist, and Harris joined several sects, including the Shakers. How to weigh these men's testimony, especially when it is their word against Joseph's, is an open question, although Cowdery and Harris's charges that Joseph was guilty of sexual unfaithfulness to his wife Emma appear to have proved true.

We will try not to rely on the evidence of unfriendly witnesses. These may be placed in two categories. In the

---

[1] Out of print, but available from Utah Lighthouse Ministries, www.utlm.org.

first category we can put pure antagonists such as E. D. Howe (*Mormonism Unvailed*), outsiders for whom Joseph can do no right. Also here belongs John Bennett, who apparently wished to use Joseph's secret teaching on plural marriage as a license for his own immorality, and who, when he became a liability to Joseph and was excommunicated, became Joseph's sworn enemy.

In another category belong those who were faithful LDS believers, but who reluctantly became opponents because they opposed Joseph's practice of plural marriage and his teachings on the plurality of gods. These include the publishers of the *Nauvoo Expositor*, and Sarah Pratt, wife of apostle Orson Pratt. These people opposed Joseph for motives similar to the *Doctrine and Covenants'* command to Oliver Cowdery to hold Joseph accountable if he ever went astray (6:18-19). To reject evidence from opponents with honest motives would appear to be blind followership to the average observer. But because such testimony is open to question, we will prefer testimony from individuals whose faithfulness to Joseph is not open to question.

How many people believed and trusted Joseph at any one time is difficult to quantify. There were large numbers of followers, but equally large numbers who fell away. While many abandoned Joseph at Kirtland for various reasons, and many were abandoning him at Nauvoo because of the reports of polygamy, many more followers came in to replace them, although most of these knew him only from afar and had not known him for long.

## Methods We Will Apply: Some Examples

During the crisis of Joseph's bank collapse in Kirtland, Ohio in 1837, according to apostle Heber Kimball, almost all of Joseph's closest followers abandoned him: "there were not twenty people on earth that would declare Joseph Smith was a prophet of God." (*Journal of Discourses* 4:108) Joseph himself confesses six years later, "Of the Twelve Apostles chosen in Kirtland, and ordained under the hands of Oliver Cowdery, David Whitmer, and myself, there have been but two what have lifted their heel against me – namely Brigham Young and Heber C. Kimball." (*History of the Church* 5:412)

Yet about a month before he died, Joseph utters this surprising sound bite: "I have more to boast of than ever any man had. I am the only man that has ever been able to keep a whole church together since the days of Adam. A large majority of the whole have stood by me. Neither Paul, John, Peter, nor Jesus ever did it. I boast that no man ever did such a work as I. The followers of Jesus ran away from Him; but the Latter-day Saints never ran away from me yet." (*History of the Church* 6:408)

What should we think of Joseph's testimony about himself in cases like this? The truth of what he says on this occasion is false, judging by the previous statement of his, confirmed (perhaps in an exaggerated statement) by Apostle Kimball, one of the two very men whom Joseph confirms remained loyal to him.

But did Joseph truly make such a boastful statement? Joseph's own *History of the Church* is as autographical a source as possible, although the text records that the sermon recorded here is a synopsis by Thomas Bullock. The historical criterion of rejection may help here. Joseph makes this statement in Nauvoo, as whispered reports about his polygamy are provoking mass defections from the church and open confrontation. Within a month, the *Nauvoo Expositor* will print its first and only edition exposing him, he will order it destroyed, and he will go to the Carthage jail where he dies. Joseph's defensive reaction to his enemies here becomes entirely plausible in view of his impending death by lynching, although the words he chooses seem to be over the top, due to stress from an increasing flood of opposition that was becoming more than he could control. Add the criterion of embarrassment, and we have words attributed to Joseph because their source sees no reason to deny them as fact.

So when Joseph gives us information, we must first check to see whether the words are really Joseph's. But then we must ask whether his words are motivated by factors that would influence what he says, and we must also verify by additional sources, if possible, whether his testimony is true.

One landmark example where Joseph's recollection of facts has been questioned is in his account of his First Vision given in the *Pearl of Great Price*, where Joseph tells that he was swayed by a citywide revival in Palmyra, New York in the year 1820. Exhaustive examination of church records and newspaper reports in the area shows plenty of specific evidence for revivals at Palmyra in 1817 and in 1824-25, but none in 1820. The 1824 revival produced ninety-nine new members at the Presbyterian church, ninety-four at the Baptist church, and 208 at the Methodist church, but in 1820, only six joined the Baptist church, and the Methodists actually lost members.[2] One can argue that Joseph simply got the date wrong, but moving the date creates problems for the rest of his narrative.

The purpose of our search for the historical Joseph is to determine whether his claim to be a prophet of God (the one who is uniquely qualified to restore God's church) is consistent with what we know about him from his words and from the testimony of those around him. We are not expecting him to be sinless; he makes no such claim, and he admits that he is a sinner like us. However, we do have a right to expect honesty and consistency from a prophet. We can hardly rely on any prophet whose life is a huge contradiction between his life and words, to tell us the truth about God on which our eternal destiny depends.

Neither do we expect to find a prophet who was divine or a performer of miracles. Joseph makes no claim to have performed miracles, nor has anyone attributed any to him, other than answers to prayer for the sick, the kind of healings that most believers see as answers to prayer in our own experience. And Joseph never claims equal rank with God, although as we saw in chapter 1, some of his followers have made him pretty central in their faith; Brigham Young reportedly dies with Joseph's name on his lips.[3] The closest that Joseph comes to such a claim is where he equates opposing him to the unpardonable sin which cannot be forgiven (*Journal of Discourses* 6:8-9).

We do want to know precisely what Joseph taught about God and other related subjects. We may look in vain to find much that Joseph actually said about the Pre-existence, although the doctrine did originate in his *Pearl of Great Price*. The same is true of his thoughts on race (see chapter 8). We will want to distinguish between actual teachings of Joseph, and doctrines which originated later, even if based on what Joseph taught.

We also want to know how reliable our sources for Joseph's words are. The LDS scriptures, Joseph's *History of the Church*, and his diaries may be considered the most reliable sources; quotes from the later LDS apostles or family members may be less reliable. And while Joseph's 1844 sermon on eternal progression (*Journal of Discourses* 6:1-11) is not straight from his own pen, it was recorded and assembled by four stenographers, and may be considered firsthand.

As we will see in chapter 9, the specifics of Joseph's theology did change and develop substantially over time. Can we attribute this to a progressive unfolding of God's truth to Joseph? What if we find later teachings that flatly contradict what he told us earlier? We will need to ponder the huge change between the Book of Mormon and the *Doctrine and Covenants* on the subject of polygamy (see chapter 7), as well as the changes between the hyper-Trinitarian theology of the Book of Mormon and the polytheistic eternal progression he teaches at the end of his life (see chapter 9).

We also must examine whether Joseph lived by his own professed revelations. This will be an important consideration in chapters 6 and 7, as we look at how Joseph observed the Word of Wisdom and his teachings on marriage. Where Joseph fails to follow them, is this a matter of the human weakness and proneness to self-contradiction that

---

[2] Wesley Walters, *New Light on Mormon Origins From the Palmyra (N.Y.) Revival* (LaMesa: Utah Christian Tract Society, 1967), 11-12.

[3] Susa Young Gates, *The Life Story of Brigham Young* (Salt Lake City: Gates, 1931), 362.

are common to us all, or are these examples of flagrant disregard? If we suspect the latter, our conclusions about whether Joseph is a prophet who can truly point us to Jesus may be impacted by how we see that.

The Bible's specific tests for a genuine prophet are whether the prophet makes predictions that prove to be false, and whether that prophet teaches a different God. (See chapter 1.) This book will not apply the test of false predictions to Joseph, both because it can be debatable whether any prophet actually made the prediction attributed to him, and because it is too easy for the prophet's faithful followers to reinterpret a prediction that does not come true as first expected. Joseph's prediction that God's temple would be built on a specific spot in Independence, Missouri (*Doctrine and Covenants* 84) has not yet come true, but one can argue that it is meant for the time of Christ's return. Similarly, when Jesus states that "this generation shall not pass away until all these things take place" (Matthew 24:34), or that "some standing here shall not taste death until they see the Son of Man coming in his kingdom" (Matthew 16:28), one may try to accuse Jesus of getting it wrong, or one may argue that exactly what he was predicting has been misunderstood.[4] I believe Jesus and Joseph must be held to the same standard; therefore, I prefer to give Joseph's predictions the same benefit of the doubt.

We can, however, test Joseph's key teachings against the Bible. Lest it be objected that many "plain and precious things" have been removed from the present Biblical text, we will deal with such objections in chapters 10 and 11. Nevertheless, we must follow the example of the believers at Berea in Acts 17:11 who "searched the scriptures daily" to see if Paul's new teachings were true. And lest it be objected that new revelations or a contemporary living prophet can set aside the clear teaching of the Bible, to make that objection, one must assume what remains to be proven, namely, that God can change his mind drastically. Rather, we must begin with the foundational assumption that any new teaching from Joseph must be consistent with what God has already spoken through the Biblical apostles and prophets.

We have seen a strong case that the historical Jesus was and is a man who taught the truth about God, practiced what he preached, and performed deeds of super-human power. He talked and acted like he was God. The evidence of his resurrection would lead us to believe that he is who he said he was. If he is not, Joseph's identity as a prophet is likewise undermined, because Joseph affirmed all the above conclusions about Jesus. But if Jesus is real, then it is important that we carefully examine Joseph to see if he is a trustworthy prophet thereof, if not the prophet to be trusted over and above other followers of Jesus who follow a very different path.

---

[4] For further examples, see my blog post "False Versus Unfulfilled Prophecy" at https://www.patheos.com/blogs/tomhobson/2018/06/false-versus-unfulfilled-prophecy/, accessed 7/23/2019.

CHAPTER 6

# JOSEPH'S APPROACH TO ALCOHOL, TOBACCO, AND "HOT DRINKS"

The principle in *Doctrine and Covenants* Section 89 to avoid tobacco, alcohol, coffee, and tea, known officially as the Word of Wisdom, is considered an important test of faithfulness by today's Latter-day Saints. Apostle Bruce McConkie once said, "Abstaining from these four things has been accepted by the Church as a measuring rod to determine in part the personal worthiness of church members."[1]

Consequently, one might be surprised to learn that Joseph Smith and his followers in the 1800's were far less strict in keeping this command than his followers today. One might be even more surprised to learn that it was only around 1906 that keeping this command became mandatory to qualify for permission to enter an LDS temple.

**What Exactly Does the Word of Wisdom Teach?**

The Word of Wisdom states that it was given as a revelation through Joseph Smith on February 27, 1833. Taking a closer look at the details, the first thing we discover is that it does not claim to be a strict command, but divine advice that is given "not by commandment or constraint" (*Doctrine and Covenants* 89:2). Instead, the Word of Wisdom describes itself as "a principle with promise" (89:2). The promise offered at the end of the chapter to those who keep these instructions is that they "shall receive health in their navel and marrow to their bones" (89:18), they shall run without growing weary and walk without growing faint (89:20), and God promises that the destroying angel shall pass by them and not slay them (89:21).

Let's take a look at exactly what this chapter actually teaches. It first declares that wine or strong drink "is not good, nor meet [acceptable] in the sight of the Father," except for the use of wine in the sacrament (89:5), and the only wine they should use on such occasions is wine "of your own make" (89:6 – 27:3 says: "you shall not purchase wine neither strong drink of your enemies," and 27:4 specifies that it should be "made new"). Otherwise, "strong drinks [which ones are not specified] are not for the belly, but for the washing of your bodies." (89:7) Curiously, 89:16-17 indicates that barley is good for "mild drinks," which could mean that beer is permitted (!), but I am aware of no one who reads the passage that way.

Next, we are told: "tobacco is not for the body, neither for the belly, and is not good for man" (89:8). Tobacco,

---

[1] Quoted in Church of Jesus Christ of Latter-day Saints, *Temple Preparation Seminar Discussions* (Salt Lake City: Corporation of the President, 1978), 68.

either smoked or chewed, is categorically prohibited except as a healing herb to be applied topically to bruises and "for sick cattle" [how, is not specified, but those "with judgment and skill" will know how to use it].

The presumed prohibition of coffee and tea actually reads: "**hot drinks** are not for the body or belly." (89:9 – emphasis added) One wishes the language had been clearer on this point! What exactly are "hot drinks"? An early LDS apostle on a mission to England spoke of how faithfully the British converts avoided "coffee, tea, and chocolate,"[2] but this is the lone bit of evidence from the time period of the Word of Wisdom that chocolate might have been included among the hot drinks intended by this prohibition. Joseph's brother Hyrum Smith declared in a sermon on the Word of Wisdom that coffee and tea are specifically what is meant.[3]

So, what else might have been intended by this prohibition? What about herbal tea? The next line in the Word of Wisdom states that "all wholesome herbs God hath ordained for the constitution, nature, and use of man" (89:10). If the use of hot water is not at issue, it would appear that herbs other than coffee or tea are permitted.

What about cold caffeinated drinks? Is the real issue the presence of stimulating drugs? (Note that the Word of Wisdom makes no mention of marijuana, cocaine, or artificial mind-altering drugs, although to argue that these are permitted by the Word of Wisdom is no doubt a misleading argument from silence.) The issue of caffeinated soft drinks was raised in 1924. When representatives of Coca-Cola convinced him that Coca-Cola contains only one-fourth the amount of caffeine found in coffee, LDS prophet Heber Grant declared that he was "sure I have not the slightest desire to recommend that the people leave Coca-Cola alone if this amount is absolutely harmless, which they say it is."[4]

Some LDS today, however, choose to be more cautious than Heber Grant about caffeinated soft drinks. An official statement by LDS church leaders states, "With reference to cola drinks, the Church has never officially taken a position on this matter, but the leaders of the Church have advised, and we do now specifically advise, against the use of any drink containing harmful habit-forming drugs under circumstances that would result in acquiring the habit. Any beverage that contains ingredients harmful to the body should be avoided."[5]

Finally, the Word of Wisdom offers some often neglected advice on the use of meat. It is to be eaten "sparingly...only in times of winter, or of cold, or famine" (89:12-13, 15). It would appear that this is the most widely ignored provision in the chapter.

How did the Word of Wisdom come about? LDS historian Leonard Arrington cites evidence that the temperance movement was exploding in size at the time this word was issued, including 239 members of the Temperance Society organized in Kirtland, Ohio on October 6, 1830 (Joseph's headquarters at the time), a group that managed to shut down two local distilleries less than a month before the Word of Wisdom was issued.[6] An article published in Alexander Campbell's magazine *Millennial Harbinger* shows that tobacco was also starting to be recognized as a threat to health at this same time; the article calls tobacco "an absolute poison."[7] Health enthusiasts of the early 1830's, including Sylvester Graham, and William Alcott, who described both tea and coffee as "poison," advocated

---

[2] Heber Kimball diary, quoted in Orson F. Whitney, *The Life of Heber C. Kimball* (Salt Lake City: Kimball Family, 1888), 165.

[3] *Times and Seasons* 3, no. 15 (June 1, 1842): 800.

[4] Heber Grant diary, quoted in Thomas G. Alexander, "The Word of Wisdom: From Principle to Requirement," *Dialogue: A Journal of Mormon Thought* 14, no. 3 (Autumn 1981): 84.

[5] Quoted in Church of Jesus Christ of Latter-day Saints, *Doctrine and Covenants Student Manual* (Salt Lake City: Corporation of the President, 1981), 209.

[6] Leonard J. Arrington, "An Economic Interpretation of the 'Word of Wisdom," *Brigham Young University Studies* 1 (1959): 39-40.

[7] Editorial, *Millennial Harbinger* 1, no. 4 (June 1830): 280.

views similar to the Word of Wisdom, including the idea that meat was a stimulant that was necessary in winter but to be avoided the rest of the year.[8]

Brigham Young's explanation of what prompted the Word of Wisdom, given in a public message on February 8, 1868, is as frank and revealing as any. He tells that Joseph held his first "school of the prophets" in his kitchen. "When they assembled together in this room after breakfast, the first thing they did is to light their pipes, and, while smoking, talk about the great things of the kingdom, and spit all over the room, and as soon as the pipe was out of their mouths a large chew of tobacco would then be taken. Often when the Prophet entered the room to give the school instructions he would find himself in a cloud of tobacco smoke. This, and the complaints of his wife at having to clean so filthy a floor, made the Prophet think upon the matter, and he inquired of the Lord relating to the conduct of the elders in using tobacco, and the revelation known as the Word of Wisdom was the result." (*Journal of Discourses* 12:158)

For the longest time, I could not figure out why today wine in the LDS sacrament has been totally replaced by water. One searches in vain to find such a change commanded anywhere in LDS authoritative writings. In December 1836, the church at Kirtland reportedly voted to ban all use of alcohol for a short time and replaced its sacramental wine with water.[9] But how and when did wine get permanently replaced by water? At the same time, how and when did the Word of Wisdom go from divine advice to strict command?

I found my answer in an excellently documented article in *Dialogue: A Journal of Mormon Thought*.[10] The changes were finalized in 1906, after a considerable debate between the presiding prophet Joseph F. Smith and his apostles. Some were in favor of strict enforcement of the ban on items forbidden in the Word of Wisdom, while some preferred leniency. Even the prophet had advised leniency toward old men who used tobacco and old ladies who drank tea.[11] The prophet's call for enforcement prevailed. Leaders at the local level began requiring strict adherence to the Word of Wisdom for those who wished to receive a temple recommend. And at that same time, wine was replaced with water in both the Temple observance of the sacrament and at the local level. (*Doctrine and Covenants* 27:2 says it does not matter what you drink in the sacrament.)

## How Strictly Did Joseph Practice the Word of Wisdom?

The church made some early attempts to enforce the Word of Wisdom. In February 1834, Kirtland LDS church leaders approved the following measure: "No official member in this Church is worthy to hold an office, after having the Word of Wisdom properly taught him, and he, the official member, neglecting to comply with it or obey it..." (*History of the Church* 2:35) Believers at Far West, Missouri went even further, declaring: "we will not fellowship any ordained member who will not, or does not, observe the Word of Wisdom according to its literal reading." (*History of the Church* 2:482) Also at Far West, Sidney Rigdon got a unanimous vote to ban stores and shops that sold liquor, tea, coffee, or tobacco. (*History of the Church* 2:524)

But Joseph Smith's personal adherence to the Word of Wisdom appears to have been more lax than the above

---

[8] See William Alcott, *Tea and Coffee* (New York: Fowler and Wells, 1836). The best collection of research on health movements surrounding the Word of Wisdom is Lester E. Bush, "The Word of Wisdom in Early Nineteenth-Century Perspective," *Dialogue: A Journal of Mormon Thought* 14, no. 3 (1981): 46-65.

[9] Matthias Cowley, *Wilford Woodruff: History of His Life and Labors* (Salt Lake City: Deseret News, 1908), 65.

[10] Thomas G. Alexander, "The Word of Wisdom: From Principle to Requirement," *Dialogue: A Journal of Mormon Thought* 14, no. 3 (Autumn 1981): 78-88.

[11] Alexander, "Word of Wisdom," 87 n5.

actions of his church would indicate. How lax? The answer depends on how much of the evidence we take to be hostile rumor, and how much we take to be reliable historical fact. As we apply the criteria of embarrassment and of multiple independent sources, we will find that at least some reports pass stringent tests of historicity, which may lend a measure of credibility to claims that we might otherwise dismiss as rumor. Whether these reports are rare exceptions to the rule in Joseph's life, or whether his failures to follow the Word of Wisdom were sufficient to deny him a modern temple recommend, is open to debate.

The dedication of the LDS temple at Kirtland, Ohio during the week of March 27, 1836 was by most accounts a wild occasion. Many visions were seen through the celebrations that week, one of which is recorded in the scripture *Doctrine and Covenants* 110. (See also Joseph's *History of the Church* 2:410-435, especially for March 29 and 30, where "we continued in the Lord's House all night," even "until five o'clock in the morning." Joseph describes the latter night as a "Pentecost.") But there were also many reports that this experience was fueled by a lot of wine being passed around by Joseph and other church leaders, albeit under arguably sacramental circumstances.[12] But these claims come mainly from Joseph's detractors and from members who are not well known to us, therefore should be regarded with skepticism.

More trustworthy is testimony about this occasion from apostle George Albert Smith, who tells that after fasting all one day that week, the brethren "got wine and bread, and blessed them…and they ate and drank, and prophesied, and bore testimony, and continued to do so until some of the High Council of Missouri stepped into the stand, and as righteous Noah did when he awoke from his wine, commenced to curse their enemies." (*Journal of Discourses* 2:216) LaMar Peterson observes that after Kirtland, rumors of drunkenness never again circulated around any activity in an LDS temple.[13]

When the Latter-day Saints at Kirtland made their mass departure in 1838, they wrote a Constitution for the group that included the provision, "no tobacco, tea, coffee, snuff or ardent spirits of any kind are to be taken internally." Joseph's brother Hyrum then addressed the group, however, and told them "not to be too particular in regard to the Word of Wisdom," possibly reflecting Joseph's point of view. (*History of the Church* 3:90, 95)

A curious incident told by LDS apostle Amasa Lyman is recorded in the diary of fellow LDS apostle Abraham Cannon. He says, "Joseph Smith tried the faith of the Saints many times by his peculiarities. At one time, he had preached a powerful sermon on the Word of Wisdom, and immediately there after [sic], he rode through the streets of Nauvoo smoking a cigar. Some of the brethren were tried as was Abraham of old."[14]

On two occasions, Joseph himself speaks of drinking wine at weddings. After one, Joseph tells us, "We then partook of some refreshments, and our hearts were made glad with the fruit of the vine. This is according to the pattern set by our Savior himself" (*History of the Church* 2:369). Two weeks later, at a wedding reception, Joseph is given "three servers of glasses filled with wine, to bless," and again, "our hearts were made glad while partaking of the bounty of earth which was presented, until we had taken our fill" (*History of the Church* 2:378).

Joseph tells us of at least two more times when he drank wine. Later in 1836, he writes that he took his mother and his aunt Clarissa to Painesville, Ohio, when they "produced a bottle of wine, broke bread, ate and drank, and parted after the ancient order, with the blessing of God." (*History of the Church* 2:447) Later on in Nauvoo, he writes

---

[12] See description in chapter 4 in LaMar Petersen, *Hearts Made Glad* (Salt Lake City: Petersen, 1975), 121-142.

[13] Petersen, *Hearts Made Glad*, 141.

[14] Diary of Abraham H. Cannon, XIX (October 1895), quoted in Gary D. Guthrie, "Joseph Smith As an Administrator" (Master's thesis, Brigham Young University, 1969), 161.

that he "called at the office and drank a glass of wine with Sister Jenetta Richards, made by her mother in England, and reviewed a portion of the conference minutes." (*History of the Church* 5:380)

Three other passages from Joseph's hand fit the historical criterion of embarrassment so well that they were edited out of his *History of the Church* by its final editors. One is where Joseph casually mentions that he "Drank a glass of beer at Moesser's." These words are found in entries to his diary published in the *Millennial Star*, but when the same page is reprinted in his *History of the Church,* these words are missing.[15] Someone must have been embarrassed.

The next passage is where Joseph writes in the same journal, "It was reported that some of the brethren had been drinking whisky that day in violation of the Word of Wisdom. I called the brethren in and investigated the case, and was satisfied that no evil had been done, and gave them a couple of dollars, with directions to replenish the bottle to stimulate them in the fatigues of their sleepless journey." When this entry was reprinted in *History of the Church*, the last two clauses after "no evil had been done" were removed.[16] Here Joseph does not drink, but he not only declares that "no evil had been done," but also gives the men money to buy more whiskey.

The final passage is found only in Joseph's handwritten diary for March 11, 1843, and was not published in the *Millennial Star* (as the two previous anecdotes were). Here the sound bite appears to be recorded by his assistant Willard Richards in the third person: "...in the office Joseph said he had tea with his breakfast. his wife asked him if [it] was good. he said if it was a little stronger he should like it better, when Mother Granger remarked, 'It is so strong, and good, I should think it would answer Both for food and drink.'"[17] All of these words were edited out when this page was reprinted in *History of the Church* 5:302.

Joseph's clerk in Nauvoo, William Clayton, assures the Saints in Europe in a magazine article that, as to reports about Joseph, "I have never seen him drunk, nor have I ever heard any man who has seen him drunk since we came here. I believe he does not take intoxicating drink of any kind: our city is conducted wholly upon temperance principles."[18]

However, Sarah Pratt, wife of apostle Orson Pratt, has a different story to tell: "A good deal of whisky was consumed in Nauvoo. Joe himself was often drunk. I have seen him in this state at different times. One evening one of the brethren brought Joseph to my home. He could not walk and had to be led by a helpful brother. The prophet asked me to make some strong coffee, which I did. He drank five cups, and when he felt he could walk a little better, he went home. He dared not come before Emma in this state. Joseph was no habitual drunkard, but he used to get on sprees."[19]

Failure to observe the Word of Wisdom appears to be a serious problem even after Joseph died. Brigham Young complains in an address at General Conference in 1872, "This people are importing perhaps more tobacco, tea, coffee and liquor than ever before during their existence as a Church... I do not mean to say that all people disregard the Word of Wisdom; but I fear that the great majority do." (*Journal of Discourses* 15:195)

In his above referenced book, LaMar Petersen packages dozens and dozens more reminiscences of violations of the Word of Wisdom by Joseph and those around him. I have focused on the few that seem to best meet the

[15] Compare *Millennial Star* 23 (1861): 720 with *History of the Church* 6:424.

[16] Compare *Millennial Star* 21 (1859): 283 with *History of the Church* 5:450.

[17] Diary of Joseph Smith, March 11, 1843, in Scott H. Faulring, ed., *An American Prophet's Record* (Salt Lake City: Signature Books, 1989), 332.

[18] *Millennial Star* 3, no. 2 (1842): 76.

[19] W. Wyl (Wilhelm Ritter Von Wymetal), *Mormon Portraits* (Salt Lake City: Tribune, 1886), 22, 27.

criteria of authenticity in illustrating Joseph's actual practice: evidence from his own words, and testimony from those friendliest to him and least likely to speak ill of him. Whether the numerous other such memories told about Joseph gain credibility from these examples (applying the criterion of coherence), and whether they together form a picture of a Joseph who often did not practice what he preached in his Word of Wisdom, is for you and I to decide for ourselves.

Should today's Latter-day Saints follow Joseph's more relaxed practice on the Word of Wisdom? Is there room for LDS leadership to change their approach to this directive? Absolutely! The LDS church can easily go back to reading the Word of Wisdom the way it was first read: as a promise of health and blessing, "not by commandment or constraint."

Is Joseph's behavior mere human weakness on his part? Or is this evidence that perhaps Joseph did not take his own revelations as seriously as others did? When we see him obey or enforce these principles, is it conscientious obedience, or is it for show? When we see him fail to observe them, is this weakness, or is this careless disregard on his part?

## What Does Jesus Say About These Issues?

The historical Jesus unquestionably drank and made wine. But through Paul his authorized representative (= "apostle"), Jesus commands us not to "be drunk" with wine (or any other mind-altering chemical) in Ephesians 5:18. Concerning tobacco, again, Jesus teaches through his apostle Paul, "I will not be enslaved by anything" (1 Corinthians 6:12*), and certainly tobacco addiction is a great slavery. Jesus comes to set us free from all that is harmful to us.

The evidence we have indicates that Jesus practiced what he preached. We have only one lone accusation from his enemies that he was a "glutton and a winedrinker" (*oinopotēs*, Matthew 11:19 = Luke 7:34), the same exaggerated source that also claims that John the Baptist "has a demon" (Matthew 11:18 = Luke 7:33). But with all the enemies that Jesus had in the Jewish and pagan world, no further such rumors materialized. The accusation appears to have arisen from Jesus' amazing willingness to dine with sinners.

We also have the testimony of one of Jesus' top three followers that "he committed no sin" (1 Peter 2:22), and Paul's declaration that Jesus is the one "who knew no sin" (2 Corinthians 5:21). If anyone could have dug up evidence for sin in Jesus' life, Paul the Pharisee would have done so. And Peter was in a position to know the truth firsthand.

CHAPTER 7

# JOSEPH'S APPROACH TO MARRIAGE

Even pro-LDS sources agree that Joseph ended up taking a large number of wives. But exactly how many wives did he take? In the cases of women who were married to other men at the time, were these marriages only spiritual? How much deception of his wife Emma and of his followers did these marriages involve? What exactly was Joseph's approach to marriage and sexual morality?

In this chapter, we will not debate the morality of polygamy, although it falls short of Genesis, Jesus, and Paul's standard: "the two [not the three or more] shall become one flesh." (See discussion in chapter 2.) What we want to focus on is the historical evidence as to whether Joseph conducted his approach to marriage consistently and in a manner worthy of a prophet of God who can be trusted to tell us the truth.

The historical testimony ranges from those who wish to deny that Joseph practiced anything other than faithful monogamy (such as the widowed Emma Smith and the RLDS Church), to those who claim that Joseph had a constant stream of one-night stands beyond what is recorded in the official record of women who were sealed to Joseph in marriage. The latter witnesses consist mostly of opponents who left his church, often precisely because of what they claim to have witnessed. We will be sparing in our use of the latter evidence.

## The Book of Mormon: Stricter Than the Bible

Did Joseph follow the Book of Mormon and his later revelation on marriage? The Book of Mormon explicitly forbids plural marriage, in terms stricter than the Bible (which does not forbid the practice). Jacob 2:24 cites the same Biblical examples that the *Doctrine and Covenants* revelation cites later when authorizing the practice: "Behold, David and Solomon truly had many wives and concubines, which thing was abominable before me, saith the Lord." The passage goes on to declare: "For there shall not any man among you have save it be one wife; and concubines he shall have none; For I, the Lord God, delight in the chastity of women. And whoredoms are an abomination before me; thus saith the Lord." (Jacob 2:27-28)

The 1835 edition of *Doctrine and Covenants* has Section 101 on marriage, which also strictly forbids polygamy: "Inasmuch as this church of Christ has been reproached with the crime of fornication, and polygamy: we declare that we believe, that one man should have one wife; and one woman, but one husband, except in case of death, when either is at liberty to marry again." The required marriage vow formula reads, "You both mutually agree to be each other's companion, husband and wife, observing the legal rights belonging to this condition; that is, keeping yourselves wholly for each other, and from all others, during your lives."[1]

---

[1] The photo-reprinted 1835 *Doctrine and Covenants* complete text is found in Wilford C. Wood, ed., *Joseph Smith Begins His Work Volume*

## Polygamy: The New Rules

Section 132 explicitly authorizes plural marriage as an ordinance of God. It was added to *Doctrine and Covenants* in 1876, while the earlier Section 101 quoted above was removed, although Section 101 remained in the book for over thirty years after plural marriage had been authorized. This revelation was not made public until after Joseph's death. The date it was reportedly "given" is July 12, 1843, but Joseph had been taking plural wives before that date, so the language was changed to "recorded" at some time after 1890. This change allows for Joseph to have received this revelation much earlier, possibly 1831 (see *History of the Church* 5: xxix).

The section begins: "Verily, thus saith the Lord unto you my servant Joseph, that inasmuch as you have inquired of my hand to know and understand wherein I, the Lord, justified my servants Abraham, Isaac,[2] and Jacob, as also Moses, David, and Solomon, my servants, as touching the principle and doctrine of their having many wives and concubines – Behold, and lo, I am the Lord thy God, and will answer thee as touching this matter. Therefore, prepare thy heart to receive and obey the instructions which I am about to give unto you; for all those who have this law revealed unto them must obey the same. For behold, I reveal unto you a new and an everlasting covenant; and if ye abide not that covenant, then are ye damned; for no one can reject this covenant and be permitted to enter into my glory." (132:1-4)

Reader, take note: Obedience to this new directive is not optional. Failure to obey brings damnation (a warning repeated in verse 6), and rejecting the practice locks you out of future heavenly glory. Finally, notice that this is to be an "everlasting" covenant, presumably one that cannot be set aside. Next, we are given the details.

This section reverses what we were told about plural marriage in the Book of Mormon: "David also received many wives and concubines, and also Solomon and Moses my servants...and in nothing did they sin save in those things which they received not from me," such as David's sin with Bathsheba. (132:38) It elaborates, "if any man espouse a virgin, and desire to espouse another, and the first give her consent,...he cannot commit adultery for they are given unto him... And if he have ten virgins given unto him by this law, he cannot commit adultery, they belong to him, and they are given to him; therefore is he justified." (132:61-62)

The revelation commands Joseph's wife, "And let mine handmaid, Emma Smith, receive all those [wives] that have been given unto my servant Joseph... But if she will not abide this commandment she shall be destroyed, saith the Lord..." (132:54)

At least four times, official church publications denied the practice of plural marriage after Joseph began to take plural wives. The *Millennial Star* tells the Saints in Liverpool in 1842, "But, for the information of those who may be assailed by those foolish tales about the two wives, we would say that no such principle ever existed among the Latter-day Saints, and never will..."[3] On September 1, 1842, to squash rumors of polygamy, the *Times and Seasons* quotes the above Section 101 of the *Doctrine and Covenants*, and states that it "is the only rule allowed by the church" (repeated on November 1), while on March 15, 1843, we read, "We are charged with advocating a plurality of wives, and common property. Now this is as false as the many other ridiculous charges which are brought against us."[4]

Both Brigham Young and William Clayton record Emma Smith's reaction to the plural marriage revelation.

---

II (Salt Lake City: Wilford C. Wood, 1962).

[2] The mention of Isaac is strange, because Genesis records Isaac as being exclusively monogamous.

[3] *Millennial Star* 3, no. 5 (1842): 74.

[4] *Times and Seasons* 3, no. 21 (1842): 909; 3, no. 23 (1842): 939; 4, no. 9 (1843): 143.

According to Clayton, when Joseph's brother Hyrum reads the revelation to Emma in hopes of persuading her to accept it, Hyrum comes back and says "he had never received a more severe talking to in his life, that Emma was very bitter and full of resentment and anger." (*History of the Church* 5: xxxii) According to Brigham, Emma asks Joseph to give her the hard copy of the plural marriage revelation. When he does so, Emma burns it. (Little does she realize that Joseph had made another copy.) Brigham said she would go to hell for rejecting it. (*Journal of Discourses* 17:159) While Emma is threatened with destruction in Section 132 if she rejects the revelation, less than a year later, Joseph is the one who was destroyed.

## Does Joseph Follow These New Rules?

Fanny Alger is the first plural wife taken by Joseph. Fanny lived with Joseph and Emma at Kirtland, Ohio. Their relationship apparently began in early 1833, when Fanny would have been sixteen.[5] Oliver Cowdery, one of the three witnesses to the Book of Mormon and the scribe to whom Joseph dictated the book, writes to his brother about Joseph's "dirty, nasty, filthy affair of his and Fanny Alger's…"[6] Joseph always denied the accusation that the two were involved together, and even excommunicated Oliver in 1838 for accusing him of adultery. Yet relatives of Fanny testify years later that Joseph asked them for permission to marry the girl, and took vows in a private ceremony.[7] But Joseph never tells or asks permission from his wife Emma. Fanny is listed on LDS church historian Andrew Jenson's official list of Joseph's plural wives.

To document all of the women that Joseph took as wives in the same detail would be beyond the scope of this present book. Jenson lists twenty-seven wives on his list.[8] Fawn Brodie documents forty-eight wives.[9] Many of these plural wives are frankly acknowledged in the LDS church's 2018 official Smith biography *Saints: The Standard of Truth*.

Yet Joseph does not even follow the rules given in the *Doctrine and Covenants* for plural marriages. At least ten of them were married women, including Mary Lightner (wife of Adam Lightner), Prescindia Buell (wife of Norman Buell), Lucinda Harris (wife of George Harris), Zina Jacobs (wife of Henry Jacobs), Nancy Hyde (wife of apostle Orson Hyde), and Patty Sessions, wife of David Sessions and mother of Sylvia Sessions Lyon (wife of Windsor Lyon), who also married Joseph. Leviticus 18:17 and 20:14 state that sex with a mother and daughter is a sex crime (*zimmah*, "wickedness"), punishable by burning all three offenders with fire. The word *zimmah* is used elsewhere in the Torah only for pimping one's daughter (Leviticus 19:29).

Were these marriages of Joseph purely spiritual, or were sexual relations involved? I will defer to the careful work of LDS researcher Todd Compton on this question,[10] but a significant amount of testimony from both some of the women themselves and from those around them reveals that Joseph spent time in bed with them.

The shock that most of the women express when first approached by Joseph indicates that these relationships were intended to be more than spiritual. Yet except for the women who lived and served in the Smith home, most

[5] Todd Compton, "Fanny Alger Smith Custer: Mormonism's First Plural Wife?", *Journal of Mormon History* 22, no. 1 (1996): 177-178.

[6] Letter from Oliver Cowdery to Warren Cowdery, January 21, 1838, Cowdery Letter Book, Docket, and Correspondence, 1833-1894, Huntington Library, San Marino, California.

[7] Compton, "Fanny," 188-197; Bushman, *Rough Stone Rolling*, 325-327; Church History Department, *Saints*, 291.

[8] Andrew Jenson, "Plural Marriage," *Historical Record* 6 (May 1887): 233-34.

[9] Brodie, *No Man Knows My History*, 457-488.

[10] Todd Compton, *In Sacred Loneliness: The Plural Wives of Joseph Smith* (Salt Lake City: Signature Books, 1997), particularly pages 12-23. Compton cites the explicit testimony of several of Joseph's plural wives that sex was involved, and that children were fathered by him under other surnames.

of these encounters were brief, with little or no further time spent by Joseph with the plural wife. Some of the relationships were ended by the furious intervention of Emma, such as the expulsion of Eliza Snow from the Smith home, indicating again that the relationships in question were more than merely spiritual.

Shock and an initial rejection of Joseph's proposal is a common theme in these encounters. Joseph asks Lucy Walker, a seventeen-year-old girl living in his home, to be his plural wife while Emma is in St. Louis: "I have no flattering words to offer. It is a command of God to you. I will give you until tomorrow to decide this matter. If you reject this message the gate will be closed forever against you." When Lucy objects that she would rather die, Joseph promises her, "God Almighty bless you. You shall have a manifestation of the will of God concerning you; a testimony that you can never deny… It shall be that joy and peace that you never knew."[11]

Joseph constantly ignored the consent requirement. Apostle Franklin D. Richards states that taking another woman without the knowledge of his wife was "fraud" and that plural marriage is without fraud when the second wife is accepted "with the mutual consent of the first." (*Journal of Discourses* 26:341) The only wives who appear to have received Emma's consent are sisters Emily and Eliza Partridge, but even here, Emma soon compelled them to leave. And while there is scanty evidence that Joseph received consent from husbands of married women, it is suggested that the husbands might have believed that they would receive a spiritual benefit or reward for their consent.

If we would follow Joseph, how do we explain numerous clear violations of all the revelations on marriage reportedly given to him? The LDS canonical revelations themselves are open to debate as to whether they came from God, but even if we grant that they came from God, how do we explain how those directives were so regularly set aside by Joseph's claims that God had given him these wives, wives that his own commands forbade him to take? Is this the God with whom we have to do, if we would follow Jesus?

At the same time, one wonders when we read all the sweet talk to Emma from Joseph up to the day he died. If there were so many other women in Joseph's life, one wonders whether that sweet talk was sincere, or simply necessary to keep from losing his one wife that everybody recognized.

## Has God Rescinded Polygamy?

Has the LDS God rescinded polygamy? Brigham Young declares, "The only men who become Gods, even the Sons of God, are those who enter into polygamy" (*Journal of Discourses* 11:269). On August 6, 1862, Brigham is quoted in Salt Lake City's *Deseret News* answering a question about why his people practice polygamy: "'And is that religion popular in heaven?' It is the only popular religion there."

But in 1890, the LDS prophet Wilford Woodruff issues a declaration now recorded in the *Doctrine and Covenants* advising Latter-day Saints "to refrain from contracting any marriage forbidden by the law of the land." How does this fit with the "new and everlasting covenant" given in 1843 with regard to marriage?

Plural marriage turns out to be an eternal principle that goes beyond the issue of whether such marriage can be practiced today. Joseph's followers taught that both Jesus and God are polygamists. Could Jesus and God be exempt from this "everlasting covenant"? Let's explore that, and see where it leads.

Dan Brown raised the issue for today's audience as to whether Jesus was married. But back in 1854, LDS apostle Orson Hyde had already ramped the issue up to an even higher level by stating in a public sermon that Jesus was a polygamist, that Mary and Martha and others were his wives, and that the wedding at Cana was his own wedding (*Journal of Discourses* 2:81-82 and 2:210 – see also 4:259).

I remember first reading this sound bite from Orson Hyde close to forty years ago, but only recently, more than

---

[11] Compton, *In Sacred Loneliness*, 458-65.

twelve years after the claims of *The Da Vinci Code*, did I connect Orson Hyde's claim with the greater debate about whether Jesus was married at all.

Brigham Young says in *Journal of Discourses* 13:309, "The Scripture says that He, the Lord, came walking in the Temple with His train; I do not know who they were, unless His wives and children; but at any rate they filled the Temple."

For me, the issue is not theological or ethical, but historical: did it really happen? Because he was the Creator incarnate, and the leading articulator of what marriage is all about, I have no problem with the hypothetical possibility of a married Jesus. Getting married could be a huge distraction from his mission (which was <u>not</u> to create a blood line of incarnate Deity!), but it would not violate his ethical standards for us, unlike a fornicating or practicing gay Jesus, which <u>would</u> violate his standards. No, my issue, plain and simple, is: Did it really happen?

I joke about it, but yet I am serious: If Jesus were married, what Jewish mother-in-law could have kept silent about it? Aside from the silence of any mother-in-law(s), the silence of the apostles is deafening. They were in the best position to know.

The most conclusive actual Scripture that makes this point is 1 Corinthians 9:5. Paul argues that he has a right to be accompanied by a wife, "as do the other apostles and the brothers of the Lord and Cephas [Peter]." So all these church leaders he cites are married. If Jesus had been married, Paul most certainly would have cited Jesus' example as his strongest argument.

Apostle Orson Pratt agrees with his fellow apostle Orson Hyde's claim that Jesus was not merely married, but a polygamist. He declares in *The Seer*, "If all the acts of Jesus were written, we should no doubt learn that these beloved women [meaning Mary, Martha her sister, and Mary Magdalene] were his wives... We have also proved most clearly that the Son followed the example of his Father, and became the great Bridegroom to whom kings' daughters and many honorable Wives were to be married."[12]

Similarly and at the same time as Pratt, Hyde, and Young made their claims, the apostle Jedediah Grant speculated, "'The grand reason why the Gentiles and philosophers of his school persecuted Jesus Christ, was, because he had so many wives; there were Elizabeth, and Mary, and a host of others that followed him... The grand reason of the burst of public sentiment in anathemas upon Christ and his disciples, causing his crucifixion, was evidently based upon polygamy, according to the testimony of the philosophers who rose in that age." (*Journal of Discourses* 1:345-346).

By implication, historic LDS apostles who claim that Jesus not only married several wives, but had earthly children by them, are creating a huge theological problem. If Jesus was God incarnate, as we in the historic Christian church believe, then he fathered children who were half-divine. But if such supposed children of his were not divine, then was Jesus not divine at this point, either? That gives us a purely human Jesus, whom we Nicene Christians categorically reject, even if he was later exalted to deity.

Pratt goes beyond today's LDS leaders by teaching that Mary the mother of Jesus was one of God the Father's wives. He writes, "We have now clearly shown that God the Father had a plurality of wives, one or more being in eternity by whom He begat our spirits as well as the spirit of Jesus His First Born, and another being upon the earth by whom He begat the tabernacle of Jesus." [13]

How can this be? Pratt argues that God "had a lawful right to overshadow the Virgin Mary in the capacity of a husband, and beget a Son, although she was espoused to another; for the law which he gave to govern men and women was not intended to govern himself...it may be that He only gave her to be the wife of Joseph while in this

---

[12] Orson Pratt, *The Seer* (reprint of the 1853-54 periodical; Salt Lake City: Utah Lighthouse Ministry, n.d.), 159, 172.

[13] Pratt, *Seer*, 172.

mortal state, and that He intended after the resurrection to again take her as one of His wives to raise up immortal spirits in eternity."[14]

Meanwhile, Pratt tells us, just as God the Father and his wives have already begotten billions of spirits to inhabit human bodies, Jesus and his wives will also beget countless millions, according to Pratt's reading of Messianic prophecies such as Isaiah 9:7 and Psalm 45:16.[15]

So already, polygamous deities (rather than a Triune God) have led to a non-virgin birth of Jesus. Today's LDS leaders do not publicly draw such conclusions, and they refuse to go the next step with Brigham Young, who publicly taught that Adam is the one who fathered Jesus in the flesh, proclaiming that Adam is "our Father and our God, and the only God with whom we have to do." (*Journal of Discourses* 1:50) In the same breath, he also emphatically states that Jesus was "*not* begotten by the Holy Ghost," with which Orson Pratt concurs.

Modern apostle Bruce McConkie probably speaks for the majority of the LDS church when he says, "In our day, the Lord summarized by revelation the whole doctrine of exaltation and predicated it upon the marriage of one man to one woman."[16] And in 2006, LDS church spokesman Dale Bills made it clear: "The belief that Christ was married has never been official church doctrine. It is neither sanctioned nor taught by the church. While it is true that a few church leaders in the mid-1800s expressed their opinions on the matter, it was not then, and is not now, church doctrine."[17]

Whether Latter-day Saints have the option to reject the teaching of a prophet of Brigham's stature is questionable from a logical standpoint. We can applaud their desire not to affirm what appear to be indefensible statements. But the LDS prophet and apostles who succeeded Joseph Smith taught a comprehensive polygamous divine order that is the logical product of *Doctrine and Covenants* 132, a divine order that cannot be so easily set aside. And what are prophets and apostles for, if they can't be taken at their word on such matters?

Joseph once said that when he was told that a prophet is always a prophet, "I told them that a prophet was a prophet only when he was acting as such." (*History of the Church* 5:265) But Brigham Young says, "I have never yet preached a sermon and sent it out to the children of men, that they might not call Scripture." (*Journal of Discourses* 13:95)

Joseph's path presents us with a choice. The choice that is most faithful to the historical Jesus is to choose the original sex and marriage ethic taught in the Book of Mormon and the 1835 *Doctrine and Covenants*, both of which confirm and clarify the original Biblical sexual ethic. The later Joseph Smith wishes to overturn that ethic, claiming that he has a new and everlasting covenant, yet we see him constantly driven to deceive his wife and his followers in order to practice that covenant. Can we trust this prophet? Is this the true God to whom he points us?

---

[14] Pratt, *Seer*, 159.

[15] Pratt, *Seer*, 172.

[16] Bruce McConkie, *Mormon Doctrine* (Salt Lake City: Bookcraft, 1966), 523.

[17] "LDS do not endorse claims in 'Da Vinci,'" *Deseret News*, May 17, 2006, online: https://www.deseretnews.com/article/635208214/LDS-do-not-endorse-claims-in-Da-Vinci.html, accessed 2/13/2019.

# CHAPTER 8

# JOSEPH'S VIEWS ON RACE

W as Joseph a racist? Even Abraham Lincoln would be considered a racist by today's standards, but how does Joseph measure up to Lincoln? The results are mixed, but there is plenty of overlooked evidence that Joseph was comparable to Lincoln, and that Joseph had a higher regard for freedom and equality for black people than he is given credit for, although some of his teachings were unfortunately used to discriminate against black people for 140 years.

## Joseph's Early Teaching: Cursed from Priesthood

The Book of Mormon sets a tone of inclusiveness for all races. It declares that God "inviteth them all to come unto him and partake of his goodness; and he denieth none that come unto him, black and white, bond and free, male and female; and he remembereth the heathen; and all are alike unto God, both Jew and Gentile." (2 Nephi 26:33)

And yet, the Book of Mormon also teaches that the Lamanites, who had been "white and delightsome," were cursed with "a skin of blackness" because of their iniquity (2 Nephi 5:21), and "cursed shall be the seed of him that mixeth with their seed" (5:23). "And the skins of the Lamanites were dark, according to the mark which was set upon their fathers, which was a curse upon them because of their transgression…this was done that their seed might be distinguished from the seed of their brethren, that thereby the Lord God might preserve his people, that they might not mix and believe in incorrect traditions which would prove their destruction." (Alma 3:6, 8) And yet, the curse appears to be conditional, one that may disappear over many generations of faith and repentance (2 Nephi 5:22, 30:6).

A few years later, Joseph's Book of Moses in the *Pearl of Great Price*, in its retelling of prehistoric Genesis, tells us, "Enoch also beheld the residue of the people which were the sons of Adam; and they were a mixture of all the seed of Adam save it was the seed of Cain, for the seed of Cain were black, and had not place among them." (Moses 7:22) In the same chapter, Enoch sees in a vision that God would "curse" the land of Canaan with much heat, "and there was a blackness came upon all the children of Canaan, that they were despised among all people." (Moses 7:8)

Also in the *Pearl of Great Price*, Joseph's Book of Abraham (1:21-27) teaches that the descendants of Ham (i.e. the African race) are under a curse that disqualifies them from holding the priesthood. (The LDS priesthood is not restricted to a select few, but is held by all males in good standing.) In this passage, the subject is Pharaoh, who is described as righteous, but who cannot hold the priesthood power that Abraham holds, because of the curse placed by Noah upon Pharaoh's ancestors.

It is alleged that this teaching was a concession to the pro-slavery crowd in Missouri during the mid-1830's when Joseph's church was being established there. Disavowing any leanings toward abolitionists of his day, Joseph writes about his views on slavery in the church magazine *Messenger and Advocate*. After citing Noah's curse on Canaan in Genesis 9, he says:

"Trace the history of the world from this notable event down to this day, and you will find the fulfilment of this singular prophecy. What could have been the design of the Almighty in this wonderful occurrence is not for me to say; but I can say that the curse is not yet taken off the sons of Canaan, neither will be until it is affected by as great power as caused it to come; and the people who interfere the least with the decrees and purposes of God in this matter, will come under the least condemnation before him; and those who are determined to pursue a course which shows an opposition and a feverish restlessness against the designs of the Lord, will learn, when perhaps it is too late for their own good, that God can do his own work without the aid of those who are not dictate by his counsel."[1]

After then discussing the New Testament teaching on slaves obeying their masters, Joseph goes on to give the following advice to his missionaries: "All men are to be taught to repent; but we have no right to interfere with slaves contrary to the mind and will of their masters. In fact, it would be much better and more prudent, not to preach at all to slaves, until after their masters are converted."[2]

In the same issue as Joseph writes the above comments, his magazine's editor, Oliver Cowdery (the scribe who recorded the Book of Mormon at Joseph's dictation), expresses a somewhat harsher view of blacks: "Where can be the common sense of any wishing to see the slaves of the south set at liberty, is past our comprehension. Such a thing could not take place without corrupting all civil and wholesome society, of both the north and the south! Let the blacks of the south be free, and our community is overrun with paupers, and a reckless mass of human beings, uncultivated, untaught and unaccustomed to provide for themselves the necessaries of life..."[3]

Oliver is concerned that abolition of slavery at this time "cannot be discussed without the sacrifice of human blood... If those who run through the free states, exciting their indignation against our brothers of the South, feel so much sympathy and kindness towards the blacks, were to go to the southern states, where the alleged evil exists, and warn those who are guilty of these enormous crimes, to repent and turn from their wickedness, or would purchase the slaves and then set them at liberty, we should have no objections to this provided they would place them upon some other continent than ours.... Certainly the people of the north have no legal right to interfere with the property of the south, neither have they a right to say they shall, or shall not, hold slaves."[4]

But in 1836, during the same year that Joseph and Oliver expressed these opinions, Joseph permitted the ordination of a black man named Elijah Abel, who was eventually ordained a member of the Quorum of Seventy in Nauvoo in 1841. Joseph knew Elijah, and hosted him in his home in Nauvoo. But Elijah, his son, and his grandson were the last black LDS men to be ordained until 1978.[5]

---

[1] *Messenger and Advocate* 2, no. 7 (April 1836): 290.

[2] *Messenger and Advocate* 2, no. 7 (April 1836): 291.

[3] *Messenger and Advocate* 2, no. 7 (April 1836): 300.

[4] *Messenger and Advocate* 2, no. 7 (April 1836): 299.

[5] For more on Elijah Abel's story, see Lester Bush, "Mormonism's Negro Doctrine: An Historical Overview," *Dialogue: A Journal of Mormon Thought* 8, no. 1 (1973): 11-68, and Newell G. Bringhurst, "Elijah Abel and the Changing Status of Blacks Within Mormonism," *Dialogue: A Journal of Mormon Thought* 29, no. 2 (1996): 109-140.

Brigham Young went on after Joseph's death to express stronger views on race than Joseph ever expressed. Brigham explicitly connects the black race with the seed of Cain: "the Lord put a mark on him, which is the flat nose and black skin. Trace mankind down to after the flood, and then another curse is pronounced upon the race – that they should be the 'servant of servants;' and they will be, until that curse is removed; and the abolitionists cannot help it, nor in the least alter that decree." (*Journal of Discourses* 7:290) With regard to intermarriage, Brigham teaches, "Shall I tell you the law of God in regard to the African race? If the white man who belongs to the chosen seed mixes his blood with the seed of Cain, the penalty, under the law of God, is death on the spot. This will always be so." (*Journal of Discourses* 10:110)

While we do find the theme of dark skin as a curse in the Book of Mormon and the Book of Moses, we look in vain for statements by Joseph as harsh as Brigham's. Unlike Brigham, Joseph has left very little explicit teaching on the subject of race, but as we will see, Joseph treats the priesthood curse as a separate issue from the fundamental worthiness of black people and their entitlement to freedom and equal rights.

## Joseph's Later Teaching: Equality and Freedom

On October 3, 1840, Joseph reports to a church General Conference in Nauvoo on the spread of the LDS message: "If the work roll forth with the same rapidity it has heretofore done, we may soon expect to see flocking to this place, people from every land and from every nation, the polished European, the degraded Hottentot, and the shivering Laplander. Persons of all languages, and of every tongue, and of every color; who shall with us worship the Lord of Hosts in his holy temple, and offer up their orisons in his sanctuary."[6] Since women did and still do worship in LDS temples, and because the subject is temple worship rather than priesthood, it is unclear whether an eventual lifting of the curse on Africans is in view, but we do see somewhat of an equalitarian slant in what Joseph says here.

In *History of the Church* 6:243, Joseph expresses his political opinion about letting Texas into the Union: "It will be more honorable for us to receive Texas and set the negroes free, and use the negroes and Indians against our foes."

Compare all of this with Joseph's equalitarian views in his Presidential campaign brochure in 1844, published in the church magazine *Times and Seasons* under the title, "General Smith's Views of the Power and Policy of the Government of the United States": "My cogitations like Daniel's, have for a long time troubled me, when I viewed the condition of men throughout the world, and more especially in this boasted realm, where the Declaration of Independence 'holds these truths to be self evident; that all men are created equal: that they are endowed by their Creator, with certain unalienable rights; that among these are life, liberty, and the pursuit of happiness,' but at the same time, some two or three millions of people are held as slaves for life, because the spirit in them is covered with a darker skin than ours."[7]

Joseph proposes some solutions: "Petition also, ye goodly inhabitants of the slave states, your legislators to abolish slavery by the year 1850, or now, and save the abolitionist from reproach and ruin, infamy and shame. Pray Congress to pay every man a reasonable price for his slaves out of the surplus revenue arising from the sale of public lands, and from the deduction of pay from the members of Congress. Break off the shackles from the poor black man, and hire them to labor like other human beings; for 'an hour of virtuous liberty on earth, is worth a whole eternity of bondage!'"[8]

---

[6] *Times and Seasons* 1, no. 12 (October 1840): 188.

[7] *Times and Seasons* 5, no. 10 (May 15 1844): 528.

[8] *Times and Seasons* 5, no. 10 (May 15 1844): 531.

Joseph zeroes in on what he sees to be the real issue, which is compensation for owners' loss of a sizable investment in their slaves: "The southern people are hospitable and noble: they will help to rid so free a country of every vestige of slavery, when ever they are assured of an equivalent for their property...were I the president of the United States, by the voice of a virtuous people, I would honor the old paths of the venerated fathers of freedom: I would walk in the tracks of the illustrious patriots,...and when that people petitioned to abolish slavery in the slave states, I would use all honorable means to have their prayers granted: and give liberty to the captive; by giving the southern gentleman a reasonable equivalent for his property, that the whole nation might be free indeed!"[9]

Which view represents Joseph's heart? One can dismiss both Joseph's appeals to Missouri slaveholders and his Presidential campaign rhetoric as merely intended for public consumption. But one suspects that "all are alike to God" (2 Nephi 26:33) is closer to what Joseph really believed. Priesthood is a side issue, compared to the issues of freedom and equality. We see this in Joseph's private conversations with Orson Hyde less than two years before he was killed, in a setting where Joseph is most likely to say what he really thinks.

When Orson Hyde asks Joseph over dinner what he would advise a convert with 100 slaves, Joseph answers, "I have always advised such to bring their slaves into a free country, set them free, Educate them and give them their equal rights."[10]

A few days later, Orson Hyde brings up the race question again after supper: "What is the situation of the Negro?" Joseph's response is: "They came into the world slaves, mentally and physically. Change their situation with the white and they would be like them. They have souls and are subjects of salvation. Go into Cincinati and find one educated [black man who] rides in his carriage. He has risen by the power of his mind to his exalted state of respectability. Slaves in Washington [are] more refined than the president."

Hyde objects, "Put them on the [same] level and they will rise above me." Joseph said, "If I raised you to be my equal and then attempt to oppress you would you not be indignant and try to rise above me?...Had I any thing to do with the Negro I would confine them by strict Laws to their own Species [and] put them on a national Equalization."[11]

Yes, Joseph speaks of a curse on the black race, but the belief that this curse was earned in a pre-existent world cannot be found in the theology we have from him. Both Joseph and Brigham expressed the tentative belief that God would someday remove the curse on black people, as we see in Joseph's warning to abolitionists in his 1836 *Messenger and Advocate* article (see above), and in Brigham's words in *Journal of Discourses* 10:250: "Ham must be the servant of servants until the curse is removed." (Brigham makes similar statements about the removal of the curse in *Journal of Discourses* 2:172, 2:184, and 7:290.)

The race issue may have been resolved by the 1978 word from the prophet that gave the priesthood to Africans, but this does not remove the question why this teaching was given in the first place. Did black people start out under a divine curse that was eventually removed by God? Or did God's prophets get it wrong on what we believe to be an important issue of faith?

---

[9] *Times and Seasons* 5, no. 10 (May 15 1844): 533.

[10] Diary of Joseph Smith, December 30, 1842, in *American Prophet's Record*, 260.

[11] Diary of Joseph Smith, January 2, 1843, in *American Prophet's Record*, 269.

## Jesus and Race

Compare Joseph with Jesus in his interaction with the Syrophoenician woman (Mark 7:24-30). In Matthew 15:21-28, she is identified as a Canaanite; we would call her Lebanese. Some today have accused Jesus of racism when he puts off the woman's request to heal her daughter with the words, "It is not fair to take the children's bread and throw it to the dogs." (Matthew 15:26*) (Notice that Luke, writing for Gentiles, does not include this episode.) The criterion of embarrassment applies, as well as the criterion of dissimilarity; it is unlike the early church to treat a Gentile this way, and although Jesus appears to be acting Judeo-centrically, his eventual willingness to grant the woman's request makes him stand out from among his fellow Jews.

I reject the claim that Jesus is supposedly facing and overcoming his own racism in this passage. Jesus is employing a rabbinic technique of using an objection to bring out a response of faith. He does not need to use this technique in the case of a similar healing request from a Roman sergeant (Matthew 8:5-10 = Luke 7:1-10), where the sergeant says that he is not worthy for Jesus to come to his house, but he knows that Jesus can give the order and it will be done. Here, Jesus marvels and says, "Not even in Israel have I found such faith!" (Matthew 8:10*)

Jesus gets a clever response of faith from the woman, a response we never would have heard if Jesus had not pushed her just a little harder than we would have: "Yes, Lord, but even the puppies eat from the crumbs falling from the table of their masters." The woman passes her test of faith with flying colors. Jesus gives the woman an A+ for her answer: "O woman, great is your faith! Be it done to you as you wish!" (Matthew 15:28*)

The reason this memory from the life of the historical Jesus was preserved and published was to counter the idea among Jesus' Jewish non-followers (which has become the predominant mindset today) that Jesus was just for Gentiles. Jesus tells the Canaanite woman, "I was not sent except to the lost sheep of the house of Israel." (Matthew 15:24 – Matthew's Jewish audience needs to hear this.) Jesus focuses on his number one priority: if you don't reach Israel first, it will be harder to reach them later. That's why Jesus instructs his followers on their mission in Matthew 10:5-6*, "Go nowhere among the Gentiles, and enter no town of the Samaritans, but rather go to the lost sheep of the house of Israel." The early church may have valued these passages because they help prove that the historical Jesus came as much for Jews as he did for Gentiles, if not more.

Only after Jesus' resurrection does Jesus shift gears and explicitly issue his Great Commission in Matthew 28:18-20*: "Go therefore and make disciples of all nations," a passage paralleled by Acts 1:8* ("You shall be my witnesses…to the end of the earth") and Mark 16:15* ("Go into all the world and preach the Gospel to the whole creation"). We have multiple witnesses from three independent sources that this too is the historical Jesus, and although one can claim that the early church invented this command to evangelize all nations, how else do we explain the Gospel's spread to all nations, unless it came from the Master himself?

Both Jesus and Joseph stand out in cultural contexts that were far more racist than our own. Both must ultimately be assessed by the results of their teachings.

# CHAPTER 9

# JOSEPH'S EVOLVING VIEWS ON GOD

We have examined Joseph's teachings and actions in numerous areas. Now, it's time to take a look at his doctrine of God, which is fundamental to any assessment we can make of him as a prophet. Is Joseph's God the true God, the one to whom Jesus pointed his followers?

Joseph's theology changed over the course of his career, from the hyper-Trinitarian theology found in Book of Mormon, to a God who is an exalted human, to the eternal progression and polytheism that Joseph proclaims in his final sermon (a message recorded by four stenographers).

Which theology should Joseph's followers believe? Doesn't the contradiction raise questions about whether we can rely on Joseph's word? And what are we to think of a God who is constantly changing? Is this the God in whom followers of Jesus are to believe?

## Hyper-Trinitarian

Today's Latter-day Saints (with the exception of the Reorganized Church) reject the Nicene Christian doctrine of the Trinity. But the Book of Mormon actually affirms <u>our</u> doctrine of the Trinity more explicitly than the New Testament itself does! In fact, I can use numerous verses from the Book of Mormon itself to defend the Biblical doctrine of the Trinity, and to refute the later teachings of Joseph Smith and Brigham Young about God.

Some of these verses express the Nicene doctrine of the Trinity exactly. For instance, in Mormon 7:7, we are told that those who are found guiltless on the Day of Judgment shall sing with the choirs above "unto the Father, and unto the Son, and unto the Holy Ghost, which are one God." 2 Nephi 31:21 says, "And now, behold, this is the doctrine of Christ, and the only and true doctrine of the Father, and of the Son, and of the Holy Ghost, which is one God, without end." Also, Alma 11:44 states that in the future resurrection, everyone shall be brought to judgment before the bar of "Christ the Son, and God the Father, and the Holy Spirit, which is one Eternal God." (See also 3 Nephi 11:27, 36.)

Other Book of Mormon passages give us clumsier, confused attempts to affirm the Christian Trinity by equating Jesus with God the Father (!) rather than saying that the two are one in substance but distinct in personality. In the third century AD, this approach (which was called Patripassionism, the belief that "the Father suffered") was rejected as well-intentioned but faulty. The closest the Bible comes to this idea is where Jesus says, "Whoever has seen me has seen the Father" (John 14:8), but the Biblical Jesus never says "I <u>am</u> the Father."

In Ether 3:14, the LDS Jesus says, "Behold, I am Jesus Christ. I am the Father and the Son." In Mosiah 16:15, we read, "Teach them that redemption comes through Christ the Lord, who is the very Eternal Father." In Alma 11:38-39, we read, "Now Zeezrom saith again unto him: Is the Son of God the very Eternal Father? And Amulek said unto him, Yea, he is the very Eternal Father of heaven and earth."

Mosiah 15:2-5 exhibits similar conflation of the persons of the triune God: "And because he dwelleth in flesh he shall be called the Son of God, and having subjected the flesh to the will of the Father, being the Father and the Son – The Father, because he was conceived by the power of God; and the Son, because of the flesh; thus becoming the Father and Son – And they are one God, yea, the very Eternal Father of heaven and of earth. And thus the flesh becoming subject to the Spirit, or the Son to the Father, being one God..."

There are numerous additional passages where the Book of Mormon declares Jesus to be the Father, or declares him to be God, far more often and explicitly than what we find in the early cautious statements in the New Testament. In addition, the Book of Mormon's Testimony of Three Witnesses ends with, "And the honor be to the Father, and to the Son, and to the Holy Ghost, which is one God." Even *Doctrine and Covenants* 20:28 states that "Father, Son, and Holy Ghost are one God, infinite and eternal, without end."

The Book of Mormon reads like a book for which the great historic Christological debates have been settled in the distant past. It reads this way, even through the mouths of characters who are supposed to be speaking hundreds of years BC.

The God of the Book of Mormon, like the Nicene Christian God, is said in Mosiah 3:5 to be the one "who was, and is from all eternity to all eternity." But Joseph Smith flatly contradicts Mosiah in a funeral sermon on April 6, 1844 when he says, "We have imagined and supposed that God was God from all eternity. I will refute that idea." (*Journal of Discourses* 6:3) In a classic sermon that is worth reading in its entirety, Joseph goes on to spell out his doctrine of eternal progression: "God himself was once as we are now, and is an exalted Man, and sits enthroned in yonder heavens. That is the great secret...and you have got to learn how to be Gods yourselves, and to be kings and priests to God, the same as all Gods have done before you..." Willard Richards quotes Joseph as saying, "I defy all Hell and earth to refute it."[1] This belief is nowhere to be found in the Book of Mormon, or in the Bible. It contradicts both.

## Bi-Theism: Two Gods of Flesh and Bone

Before we go there, however, Joseph's theology passed through an interim stage we might call bi-theism. (Or tri-theism, although little attention is paid to the divine status of the Holy Ghost here.) This view is based on the 1838 *Pearl of Great Price* version of Joseph's First Vision of the Father and the Son. Here is where Joseph at age fourteen (1820) goes out into the woods to seek God on the question of which church he should join, where he sees "two Personages," one of whom says to him, "*This is My Beloved Son. Hear Him!*" (Joseph Smith 2:17, emphasis original)

In an earlier version of Joseph's story, printed in the *Deseret News* on May 29, 1852, Joseph calls this event his "first visitation of angels," which was changed to "my first vision" when this version was reprinted in *History of the Church* 2:312. In a still earlier version (dated to 1831-1832) in Joseph's own handwriting, Joseph writes that when he was "in the 16th year of my age...I saw the Lord and he spake unto me saying Joseph my son thy sins are forgiven thee... I am the Lord of glory I was crucifyed [sic] for the world..."[2] Still another version is found in Joseph's diary for 1835-1836, where Joseph writes that an unidentified "personage" appears to him in a pillar of fire, then "another

---

[1] Quoted in Faulring, ed., *American Prophet's Record*, 341.

[2] See Dean C. Jessee, "The Early Accounts of Joseph Smith's First Vision," *Brigham Young University Studies* 9, no. 3 (1969): 275-294. The hard copy version contains a photograph of the document on page 281.

personage soon appeared like unto the first, he said unto me thy sins are forgiven thee, he testifyed [sic] unto me that Jesus Christ is the Son of God; and I saw many angels in this vision I was about 14 years old when I received this first communication."[3] A fifth version is reported by Brigham Young, who says, "The Lord did not come with the armies of heaven... But He did send His angel to this same obscure person, Joseph Smith jun....and informed him that he should not join any of the religious sects of his day, for they were all wrong..." (*Journal of Discourses* 2:171)

The versions disagree strongly as to exactly who appeared to Joseph: whether it was both Father and Son, or Jesus only, or angels. Whether the different accounts can be reconciled, others may decide, but a lot of theological freight hangs on whether the 1838 version is true. LDS apostle Gordon Hinckley declares, "If the First Vision [he means the official version] did not occur, then we are involved in a great sham. It is just that simple."[4]

If we accept the official version, the most important contribution of the official First Vision account is the portrayal of both Father and Son as bodies of flesh. By implication, the Christian understanding of the Trinity is hereby replaced by two separate gods. The teaching that God has a body of flesh and bones, which has become the standard teaching of the LDS church down to this day, also contradicts Joseph's Lectures on Faith printed in the 1835 version of the *Doctrine and Covenants*.

The Lectures on Faith already reject the Christian doctrine of the Trinity. In the Q & A section for Lecture 5 (page 55), we read: "Q. How many personages are there in the Godhead? A. Two: the Father and the Son." But in the same Lecture (page 53), we find that God is said to be "a personage of spirit," while the Son is "a personage of tabernacle" and "is called the Son because of the flesh," while the Spirit is only the "mind" they share. Also, in Lecture 2 (page 26), we are told that God is "omnipresent," implying that he cannot have a body of flesh.[5] But by 1838, Joseph teaches that God the Father has a body of flesh, which helps explain why the Lectures on Faith were removed from the *Doctrine and Covenants*.

The vision of God the Father with a human body of flesh is particularly important, because it paves the way for Joseph's teaching that God is a glorified, exalted human who progressed to divine status. Like countless ancestors before him, Joseph's God starts out as a human being, becomes God, and is now in the process of becoming an even greater being.

## Gods Unlimited

Joseph starts referring to Gods (plural) in the Book of Moses and Book of Abraham in the *Pearl of Great Price*. He clearly rejects the Christian Trinity by now: "Many men say there is one God; the Father, the Son and the Holy Ghost are only one God! I say that is a strange God anyhow—three in one, and one in three! It is a curious organization." (*History of the Church* 6:476)

Joseph says in his final sermon (June 16, 1844) that he's been preaching this all along. "I will preach on the plurality of Gods. I wish to declare I have always and in all congregations when I have preached on the subject of the Deity, it has been the plurality of Gods. It has been preached by the Elders for fifteen years. I have always declared God to be a distinct personage, Jesus Christ a separate and distinct personage from God the Father, and that the Holy Ghost was a distinct personage and a Spirit, and these three constitute three distinct personages and three Gods." (*History of the Church* 6:474)

---

[3] Diary of Joseph Smith, November 9, 1835, in *American Prophet's Record*, 5-6.

[4] Gordon B Hinckley, *Teachings of Gordon B. Hinckley* (Salt Lake City: Deseret, 2016), 227.

[5] See the reprinted version in Wood, *Joseph Smith Begins His Work Volume II*.

But in his King Follett funeral sermon on April 6, 1844, Joseph unpacks a full-blown polytheism, including a God who was not God from all eternity, who did not have the power to create human spirits, and who did not create the universe from nothing, but merely organized pre-existing matter. He also declares that God, intelligence, and human souls are all self-existent and co-equal, and that matter has no beginning or end and has existed for as long as God has existed. See what he says, according to *Journal of Discourses* 6:8:

"The mind or the intelligence which man possesses is coequal with God himself. I know that my testimony is true; hence, when I talk to these mourners, what have they lost? Their relatives and friends are only separated from their bodies for a short season: their spirits which existed with God have left the tabernacle of clay only for a little moment, as it were; and they now exist in a place where they converse together the same as we do on the earth. I am dwelling on the immortality of the spirit of man. Is it logical to say that the intelligence of spirits is immortal, and yet that it had a beginning? The intelligence of spirits had no beginning, neither will it have an end. That is good logic. That which has a beginning may have an end. There never was a time when there were not spirits; for they are co-equal with our Father in heaven."

Here are some extracts from the reporter's notebook on what Joseph said that day, as recorded by Wilford Woodruff, fourth prophet of the LDS church:

"The Gods came together & concocked [sic] the plan of making the world & the inhabitants...the learned Dr says the Lord made the world out of nothing, you tell them God made the world out of something, & they think you are a fool. But I am learned & know more than the whole world, the Holy Ghost does any how, & I will associate myself with it."[6] [Joseph then mistranslates "beaureau" (Hebrew *bara'*, which actually means "to create out of nothing") as "to organize the world out of chaotic matter."] Joseph goes on: "The soul of man, whare [sic] did it come from? The learned says God made it in the beginning, but it is not so, I know better God has told me so. If you don't believe it, it wont make the truth without effect, God was a self exhisting [sic] being, man exhists upon the same principle...man exhisted in spirit & mind coequal with God himself...Intelligence is Eternal and it is self exhisting..."[7]

William Clayton was also taking notes that day: "Another subject – the soul – the mind of man – they say God created it in the beginning. Don't believe the doctrine – know better – God told me so... We say that God was self-existant [sic] who told you so? It's correct enough but how did it get into your heads – who told you that man does not exist upon the same principle... The mind of man – the intelligent part is coequal with God himself. I know that my testimony is true. hence when I talk to these mourners what they have lost – They are only separated from their bodies for a short season but their spirits existed coequal with God..."[8] In Clayton's version, we read, "...God never did have the power to create the spirit of man at all. He could not create himself – Intelligence exists upon a selfexistent principle."[9]

Joseph's earliest successors proceed to take his teaching and run with it. We see Joseph's universe in the following quotes from Brigham Young:

---

[6] Text in Faulring, ed., *American Prophet's Record*, 345.

[7] Faulring, *American Prophet's Record*, 345-346.

[8] Text in Faulring, ed., *American Prophet's Record*, 359.

[9] Faulring, *American Prophet's Record*, 360

- "How many Gods there are, I do not know. But there never was a time when there were not Gods and worlds, and when men were not passing through the same ordeals that we are now passing through." (*Journal of Discourses* 7:333)
- "...man is the king of kings and lord of lords in embryo" (*Journal of Discourses* 10:223)
- "...the God that I serve is progressing eternally, and so are his children: they will increase to all eternity, if they are faithful" (*Journal of Discourses* 11:286)

Apostle Orson Pratt sees a similar vision of the universe proposed by Joseph Smith: "We were begotten by our Father in Heaven; the person of our Father in Heaven was begotten on a previous heavenly world by His Father; and again, He was begotten by a still more ancient Father; and so on, from generation to generation..."[10] Pratt guesses, "If we should take a million of worlds like this and number their particles, we should find that there are more Gods than there are particles of matter in those worlds" (*Journal of Discourses* 2:345).

How does one reconcile such unlimited polytheism with the LDS claim that there is only "one God with whom we have to do"? Orson Pratt makes a valiant attempt, although it is foreshadowed in Joseph's teaching on the subject. Pratt proposes a sort of pantheism, theorizing that the millions of gods past and present are all part of one God, along with us (since we are gods in embryo).[11]

The Bible rejects such polytheism categorically. Joseph's God is a very different God than the God of Isaiah 43:10* and numerous other verses, where God says clearly, "Before me was there no God formed, neither shall there be after me." Isaiah 45:22: "I am God, and there is no other." Deuteronomy 4:39*: "The Lord is God in heaven above and on the earth beneath: there is no other." Joel 2:27*: "I, the Lord, am your God, and there is no other."

## Can God Change So Drastically?

Does God change, or does God remain forever the same? Malachi 3:6 (KJV) says, "For I am the Lord; I change not." Hebrews 13:8 tells us that "Jesus Christ is the same yesterday, and today, and forever." Jesus was born as one of us at Bethlehem, but he was always co-eternal with God. Even the Book of Mormon says, "For I know that God is not a partial God, neither a changeable being; but he is unchangeable from all eternity to all eternity." (Moroni 8:18)

A related question: Can God change his mind or his plan? Can God change his rules, or is everything that God decrees an expression of unchanging divine principle? Joseph's God is very capable of changing his mind on major issues, as we see in the 1978 revelation giving the priesthood to all worthy male Africans, and even during Joseph's own lifetime, as we see rapid changes in what his God reveals in his inspired writings.

But didn't God change the rules about kosher food in Leviticus 11 and Deuteronomy 14? When Jesus taught that nothing that goes into a person defiles him/her, Mark argues that Jesus thereby "declared all foods clean" (Mark 7:14-19). Similarly, Paul writes, "I know and am persuaded in the Lord Jesus that nothing [meaning food] is unclean in itself" (Romans 14:14*).

Some of God's laws given through Moses were only intended for Israel, but some are timeless and universal. How can we tell which is which? One way is to see which laws are reaffirmed in the New Testament. Another way is to see how severe are the penalties for disobeying those laws. The New Testament does not reaffirm the laws about clean and unclean, but it reaffirms the Ten Commandments. I have explored this further in my book, *What's on God's Sin List for Today?* (Eugene: Wipf and Stock, 2011)

[10] Pratt, *Seer*, 132.

[11] See discussion in Pratt, *Seer*, 132.

Can God change his mind (= repent)? We are told that God "was sorry" (*niham*) to have made the human race in Genesis 6:6, that God "was sorry" to have made Saul king (1 Samuel 15:11), and that God "changed his mind" about destroying Israel (Exodus 32:14) and Nineveh (Jonah 3:10), all using the same word. But the Bible also says that God is not a human being, that he should repent (same word – see Numbers 23:19, 1 Samuel 15:29).

The same word can and does cover both meanings. Should we suppose that God did not know what would happen under Plan A, so God changes his mind to a better plan? Speaking as a Calvinist myself, I prefer to think that God's mind does not change, but that God enacts first one course of action (Plan A) that God knows will be disastrous, then switches to a better course of action (Plan B), purely by sovereign choice, to prove what would happen under Plan A.

Does the Calvinist solution sound complicated? To me, it sounds a lot better than the prospect that God keeps making bad decisions that have to be changed. How do you make a deal with a God who can't be counted on to keep promises? If those promises were conditional, we can understand why they would be withdrawn, but we would not accept such withdrawn promises if they were mistakes in planning on God's part.

Joseph Smith ends his earthly life with a fundamentally different concept of God than the God he started out with. How the two are compatible is difficult if not impossible to explain. It is also hard to see how the Book of Mormon contains "the fullness of my everlasting gospel," as claimed in *Doctrine and Covenants* 27:5, if Joseph's teaching about God at the end of his life is true.

Personally, I do not believe the story told by the Book of Mormon. But for those who do believe the book, I would urge them to believe in the triune God taught in the Book of Mormon, rather than in the later teachings of Joseph Smith and his successors. And if the choice between these two Gods is difficult, I would ask them to consider whether their leaders have strayed from the truth, and whom they should follow when forced to make such a choice.

## CHAPTER 10

# Joseph's Far-Reaching Claims

### Pre-existence: Is There a Case for It?

Joseph makes some far-reaching claims that one can only take on faith. For instance, the claim that humans existed in a spirit world before we born on earth is a major feature of today's LDS faith. It is their answer to the question, "Where do I come from?"

Joseph himself said surprisingly little about the Pre-existence. He introduces the idea in his *Pearl of Great Price*. In Moses 3:5-7, where Joseph gives his retranslation of early Genesis, God says that he created all things "spiritually, before they were naturally upon the face of the earth," including human beings. In Abraham 3:21-28, God shows to Abraham "the intelligences that were organized before the world was," including "many noble and great ones," and God approves a proposal to create an earth where they may be put to the test. Those who "keep their first estate" will enjoy glory in a higher kingdom than those who do not.

Let's examine Joseph's teaching on the Pre-existence to see how it measures up to God's word in the canonical Bible. In so doing, we will be turning to a leading LDS authority who spoke more in detail on this subject.

LDS theology teaches that God the Father dwells near a star called Kolob (Abraham 3:2-4 – namesake of a canyon in Zion National Park) with an unspecified number of wives, where he is procreating multitudes of spirit children who must wait until they are implanted into bodies of flesh to be born on earth. We do not remember this existence, but it becomes an incentive for LDS families to have as many children as possible, so that a maximum number of spirit children will have maximum opportunity to accept the LDS message.

In the mid-1800's, LDS apostle Orson Pratt (mathematician, scientist, and early chancellor of the University of Utah) devoted much attention to making the case in favor of the doctrine of the Pre-existence. He makes his case in his volume *The Seer* and in *Journal of Discourses* 21:197-206.

Pratt insists that spirits are begotten, not created. He rejects the possibility that God creates each person's spirit when he/she is conceived; that would require God to be working too hard to say that he rested from his work of creation. Pratt thinks that eternal procreation would avoid this problem. But if it is overwork to create billions of spirits, isn't it just as much overwork to beget billions of them? Even Solomon and his oversized harem would appear to be unequal to such a task.

Pratt's Biblical argument begins with Ecclesiastes 12:7, where we are told that the human spirit "returns to God who gave it." Pratt asks, "Could the spirit *return* to God, if it never were in His presence? Could we return to a place where we never were before?"[1] He also points to our innate knowledge of God and of moral law as evidence that we learned it in a previous existence.

Pratt cites the disciples' question to Jesus about the man born blind in John 9:2 as proof that both Jesus and his followers presume a previous existence. He quotes Hebrews 12:9, where we are told that God is the "Father of spirits" (in contrast to the "fathers of our flesh"). He also cites Job 38:4-7, where God asks Job, "Where were you…when the morning stars sang together, and all the sons of God shouted for joy?" (Curiously, he does not add Jeremiah 1:5, "Before I formed you in the womb, I knew you.")

Pratt also injects into his picture of the Pre-existence an element of karma that the belief itself does not demand. He points out that some spirits are born into places where they are more likely to hear and believe the LDS message than others are. He also observes that some are born into the African race, which was declared to be under a curse by Brigham Young and the Book of Abraham. Pratt then asks, "Now if all the spirits were equally faithful in their first estate in keeping the laws thereof, why are they placed in such dissimilar circumstances in their second estate?"[2] If one accepts Pratt's premises, the LDS Pre-existence resembles an abbreviated form of reincarnation, with only one previous life (as it were) before the present one.

Needless complications are raised by predicating this pre-mortal existence. Like the problem with reincarnation, why should we be punished for sins that we don't remember? What's worse is the idea that Africans were born under a curse because they were not righteous in this Pre-existence. While this curse was declared to be lifted in the 1978 revelation, how does one remove the LDS scriptural claim on which the curse was based?

The Bible refutes the belief that human spirits must be procreated by God rather than created within the unborn child. In Genesis 2:7, we are told that God breathed into us the breath of life. In Zechariah 12:1, God states that he is the one "who formed the human spirit within." And in Psalm 139:13-16 (see also Isaiah 44:24), God's intimate involvement in the formation of human embryos contradicts Pratt's argument that God cannot devote enough time and effort to the creation of billions of human spirits as well.

We can also correct the misinterpretation of the verses used to support the LDS belief in the pre-mortal spirit world. Before birth, Jeremiah (and the rest of us) existed only in the mind of God, not as pre-mortal spirits. God's question to Job "Where were you?" has a better answer: you did not exist! Likewise, Pratt's appeals to Ecclesiastes 12:7 and John 9:2 do not prove what he thinks those verses prove.

The only person in Scripture who actually did exist before his life in the flesh is Jesus Christ, to which John 1:30, 8:58, and 17:5 and Colossians 1:17 bear witness. However, these verses cannot be applied like Pratt does to teach the pre-existence of other human spirits. Jesus says that he is the only one who has seen the Father in any previous world (John 6:46).

How does God create our spirits? Does it happen through special creation, or do we get them from our parents? Christian theologians have leaned toward the first option, but even if God uses the spirits of our parents to create our spirits, the end product is a new creation, just as surely as God uses the DNA of our parents to create a totally new body.

Not only does the Bible reject the concept of our pre-existence, but we are better off without it. The love between a husband and wife is a far cry from the duty to procreate thousands of spirit children. And while the LDS Pre-existence explains the circumstances of our birth to be an achievement of our own merit in our previous existence, the Bible puts the circumstances of our birth entirely in the hands of a sovereign God.

---

[1] Pratt, *Seer*, 17.

[2] Pratt, *Seer*, 56.

## Adam in Missouri? Show Me

Joseph makes another far reaching claim that we are forced to take or reject on faith: the claim that Adam was a (life long?) resident of Missouri. Adam-ondi-Ahman is the place in northwestern Missouri where we are told that Adam and his descendants gathered for a final blessing before Adam's death (*Doctrine and Covenants* 107:53). It is also the place where Adam will return to visit his people in a global event at some unspecified time in our future (*Doctrine and Covenants* 116). According to later LDS sources, Joseph Smith taught that the Garden of Eden was in Independence, Missouri, and that when Adam was driven out of the Garden, he built an altar at Adam-ondi-Ahman.

The modern site of Adam-ondi-Ahman is a beautiful section of woodland and fields near Jameson, Missouri that overlooks the Grand River. It was originally called Spring Hill. The land is now owned by the LDS Church. There is no visitor center or any tourist fanfare; perhaps the lack of publicity is good for a site considered to be sacred. Also included in the site is Tower Hill, where Joseph Smith states that he discovered stones from an old Nephite altar (*History of the Church* 3:35). The stones on display at the site are not claimed to be the ones Joseph saw, but they come from the right area, so who knows?

Joseph Smith began to build a town here in 1838, and planned to build a temple. However, as the town grew to over 1000, a local militia/mob drove them to evacuate both Adam-ondi-Ahman and Far West, a larger LDS settlement thirty-five miles to the south, where four foundation stones were laid for another proposed temple. Violence against Joseph's followers culminated in the hideous Haun's Mill massacre, which shocked the rest of Missouri, after which the LDS made their move to Nauvoo, Illinois.

Today, despite the thousands who once gathered in these two places, virtually no signs of settlement remain at either site, other than the temple foundation stones at Far West. It is easy to understand why today's Latter-day Saints often interpret any attempts to oppose or convert them as being more of what they endured in Missouri. Whatever motives may have been involved, the violence inflicted on Joseph's followers in Missouri did not advance the cause of truth.

To believe that Adam came to Missouri is a leap of faith. But it is just as much a leap of faith to believe that he lived in Mesopotamia, let alone to believe in the existence of an historical Adam of any kind. Genesis does not specify where the land of Nod ("Wandering") was to which Adam and Eve went when exiled from the Garden of Eden, but Genesis does specify that the Garden itself stood at the junction of the Tigris, Euphrates, and two other ancient rivers. One must choose between the Bible's location for Adam, and the claims of Joseph Smith, which drives home the question of whom we regard as our ultimate authority, in the absence of further evidence.

One must also be sure that the reports on what those sources say are reliable. How do we know what Joseph Smith really taught about Adam in Missouri? The most reliable reports are those that come from Joseph's own pen: reports from the *Doctrine and Covenants*, and from his *History of the Church* (based on his own diary). Less reliable are reports from his apostle Heber Kimball, from the fourth LDS prophet Wilford Woodruff, and from Joseph Fielding Smith, the sixth LDS prophet, who was a nephew of Joseph himself and who was born at Far West, Missouri. If one subtracts the secondary reports, we have no Garden of Eden in Missouri, only an alternative site for the Land of Nod to which Adam and Eve were driven, a teaching that does not contradict the teaching of Genesis.

Whomever we choose to believe when such a claim is made, we must make sure we know the truth about the one on whose words we are betting our soul. I find the Bible to stand head and shoulders above any other voice that claims to speak for God. The Bible's narrative is confirmed by amazing discoveries such as Sennacherib's own version of his war with Hezekiah (2 Kings 18:13-16), the Moabite Stone (where King Mesha gives his own version of his war with Israel in 2 Kings 3:21-27), and Hezekiah's inscription marking his completion of a 1700-foot water tunnel (2 Kings 20:20).[3] There is so much hard evidence to back up what the Bible says, that even in places where evidence is lacking, such as the question of Adam in Missouri, I am compelled to give the Bible's word the benefit of the doubt.

Adam in Missouri? The Missouri state motto is: "Show Me." We must let evidence and reliable testimony lead us to the source of truth on which we can build our lives.

## The Great Apostasy

The huge central faith claim made by Joseph and the Book of Mormon that comes from his hand is his claim about the Great Apostasy: true Christianity ceased to exist after the end of the first century AD, only to be restored in the latter days (ours) by divine initiative through Joseph Smith.

The first question we must ask is whether this predicted Great Apostasy would be total. If the true church did not totally cease to exist, it would not need a total restart on the scale taught by Joseph. But the Bible teaches, not a total future apostasy, but only a partial one: "Now the Spirit expressly says that in the latter times *some* shall depart from the faith." (1 Timothy 4:1*) "Then *many* will fall away / be offended" (literally "scandalized" – Matthew 24:10*).

## Has Anything "Plain and Precious" Been Removed?

This falling away from the truth taught by Joseph was reportedly made possible in part through major revisions of the Bible and its teachings. As 1 Nephi 13:28 puts it, "Wherefore, thou seest that after the book hath gone forth through the hands of the great and abominable church, that there are many plain and precious things taken away from the book, which is the book of the Lamb of God."

Is the Book of Mormon's charge true? Who chose the books of the Bible? And what got left out, and why? Contrary to the claims of *The Da Vinci Code*, there was no top-down decree or official vote on the books of either the Old Testament or New Testament. The identification of which books were God's word was a grassroots effort, a process that took place over time.

There are two ways we can tell which books people believed to be authoritative. One way is by popular usage: which books keep getting used or quoted as the word of God. The other way is when people make official lists, which at least give us the opinions of the people who made the lists.

For the Old Testament, Protestant Christians have simply accepted the unanimous Jewish opinion on which books were Scripture. The Catholics and Orthodox also accept the books that were included in Greek copies of the Old Testament, books which the Jews never treated as sacred. Josephus (end of first century AD) tells us that copies of each book of Holy Scripture were kept in the Temple before it was destroyed. Josephus is the first to give us a list of those books, which contains the same books as we have in our Hebrew canon. There is much more that can be said, but there was nothing sneaky about the process.

The consensus around 180 AD about the New Testament canon (as we see in a text called the Muratorian Canon) was very close to what appears on canon lists in the late 300's (the lists in the late 300's are where we get the list we have today). If anything, the early church before 300 AD leaned toward leaving out books that we have included. A lot of early writers never quote James or 2 Peter. The list from 180 AD leaves out Hebrews, James, 1-2

---

[3] For a divinity-school-level course full of such evidence, I recommend K. A. Kitchen, *On the Reliability of the Old Testament* (Grand Rapids: Eerdmans, 2003). Kitchen was a leading expert on Pharaoh Ramesses II and professor of Egyptology at the University of Liverpool.

Peter, and 3 John, plus it includes Wisdom (from the Old Testament Apocrypha!) and the Apocalypse of Peter (although the writer says some will not allow it to be read in church).

So, how did the early church decide what books could be trusted? For instance, how did they narrow it down to four Gospels and no others? We owe a tremendous debt to Christians who lived around 70-100 AD. They were the ones who could still remember what Jesus said and did, so they were in the position to know which books told the truth about Jesus. Luke was probably a major player in collecting these books.

The early church used four criteria to determine what belonged in their Bible: 1. Apostolicity (did it come from an apostle or someone close to the apostles who preached the same message?). 2. Antiquity (is it old enough to really go back to the apostles?). 3. Orthodoxy (does it fit with what we already know is true about Jesus?). 4. Usage (is everybody quoting it?).

Notice that the four Gospels are anonymous (there are no names in the text themselves – these books didn't need titles to prove that they were apostolic), while the fake books relied on name recognition, which still failed to win acceptance for Peter and Thomas. An apostolic name on the label was no substitute for content; if the content is junk, so is the name on the label.

Pseudonymity (writing under false names) was a unique issue for Christians, because it impacted apostolicity. If a book claims to have been written by Peter or Paul, but it wasn't, it's not apostolic. The early church was not gullible. They were slow to accept 2 Peter as genuine, and many did not accept the Epistle to the Hebrews, on the grounds that they did not believe it was written by Paul. (But Hebrews never claims to be by Paul. I believe that it was written by Apollos of Alexandria, a guy who hung out with Paul and preached the same message.)

So if we had closed the New Testament canon around 200 AD, not all the books we have today would have made the cut. But early believers were unanimous in rejecting almost all of the books that never made it into our Bibles. This was not a top-down decree from some ruler or council. It was a grassroots effort, a process over time in which the whole group participated.

So who got cut out of the New Testament by the earliest believers, and why? There are two categories of books that did not make the cut. The first category is the books that were considered to be false teaching or heretical, which includes the so-called Gnostic writings. These include the *Gospel of Peter* (where Jesus stomps out of his tomb with his head in the clouds), the *Gospel of Thomas*, the "Infancy Gospels," the *Gospel of Mary*, the *Gospel of Judas*, and the second *Apocalypse of Peter*.

By the way, the Gnostic writings were not suppressed, as Bart Ehrman and Dan Brown would have you believe. The content of these books has been an open secret for over 1,800 years. Early Christians would yell, "Bad book! And here's what it says!" So when forty-six Gnostic books were unearthed at Nag Hammadi, Egypt, we found that the early church was telling us the truth about these books that they allegedly suppressed.

Bart Ehrman is wrong when he claims that the Gnostics were victims. He thinks the early church probably had what we would call heretical beliefs, and that we "won," not because we were right, but because we had the muscle to stomp out our competitors. No, the Gnostics were not oppressed underdogs; they were elitists. Both the Gnostics and the orthodox would have rejected the idea that both of them could be right. And nobody was in the position to force one conclusion or the other down anyone's throats. Grassroots believers decided that the Gnostic books were bogus as a source of truth about Jesus.

So what was wrong with these books, then? The Gnostics believed that the material world was evil. They believed there were two gods: the evil creator God of the Old Testament, and the New Testament god of sweetness and light. Marcion (140 AD) was one of the first famous teachers of this heresy, although Gnosticism was already well under way in the 90's, if not earlier. Marcion and the Gnostics threw out the whole Old Testament, and

Marcion did a chop job on the New Testament as well, leaving only a mutilated copy of Luke, and ten letters of Paul with everything Jewish cut out of them.

The Gnostics believed that Jesus was just a ghost. He appeared to be human, but he was not part of the material world. The Gnostics believed they had secret teachings of Jesus to help them rise above the material world. In earlier books, like the *Gospel of Peter* and the *Gospel of Thomas*, the weird teachings are comparatively mild, but as time went on (past 200 AD), Gnostic teaching got more complicated. As we saw in chapter 3, the Jesus of the Infancy Gospels is a holy terror who pronounces fatal curses on any playmate who crosses him up. In the so-called *Acts of John*, Jesus never left footprints. In the *Second Apocalypse of Peter*, the speaker sees someone nailed to the cross, and someone above the cross, glad and laughing; the one who is glad and laughing above the cross is the living Jesus, and the one on the cross is just a substitute. Christians could tell this was a very different Jesus than the one found in the books that they could trust. No less an LDS authority than apostle James Talmage agrees that these books were false.[4]

The other books that didn't make the cut were good books that came along too late to make the publication deadline. These books show us what the early church really believed. There is nothing off-base or bizarre in them, but there is also nothing essential in them that is not already found in the Bible, and the authors are not apostles who lived in Jesus' day. So the guy who wrote the list in 180 AD says that the *Shepherd of Hermas* is a good book, but it's too recent to be an authority for their faith. Other such books include *1-2 Clement*, the letters of Ignatius, *Barnabas*, and the *Didachē*, all written from 95-130 AD.

Were there LDS books that were suppressed? There is no trace of such books, and from what we have seen, such books would have been extremely hard to extinguish if they had existed. The Book of Mormon's claim that "plain and precious" elements were removed from God's word is unsubstantiated, both on the level of which books were included, and on the level of the text and translation of the books that the Nicene and LDS churches both accept.

## Translated Correctly?

Article 8 of the LDS Articles of Faith states, "We believe the Bible to be the word of God as far as it is translated correctly." So the LDS church accepts the Bible, with an open-ended exception. But Article 8 immediately goes on to accept the Book of Mormon, without exception.

So what exactly is the LDS church's problem with our translation of the Bible? Is the Bible reliable? At the points where the LDS church and Nicene Christianity disagree on Biblical teachings, the Latter-day Saints can claim that "plain and precious" Biblical teachings were either left out or changed.

So the issues are: 1. the reliability of the Biblical text, and 2. how to translate the text we have. Neither of these issues is thorny enough to substantiate the LDS claims that our debates about doctrine are due to either textual alteration or mistranslation. Let's look at the evidence.

Joseph Smith says on October 15, 1843, "I believe the Bible as it read when it came from the pen of the original writers. Ignorant translators, careless transcribers, or designing and corrupt priests have committed many errors." (*History of the Church* 6:57) Apostle Bruce McConkie agrees with Joseph as he speaks for the modern LDS church: "Many passages and even whole books of scripture have been lost through the carelessness or wickedness of the record keepers."[5] We have already addressed the issue of books being removed. Now, let's take a look at the questions of text and translation.

---

[4] James E. Talmage, *The Great Apostasy* (Salt Lake City: Deseret, 1978), 98-99.

[5] McConkie, *Mormon Doctrine*, 453.

How reliable is our text of the Bible? Centuries of uncontrolled copying that happened before the Old and New Testament texts were semi-"standardized" may be seen as both a curse and a blessing. The curse is obvious: hundreds of pesky variations. But the vast majority of these variations are comparatively minor, and do not endanger the basic content of the text.

In fact, no textual issue in the Bible puts any important teaching of the Bible at risk. For example, there are places in the New Testament such as John 1:18, Acts 20:28, and 1 Timothy 3:16 where copyists tried to alter our belief that Jesus is God, but those attempted alterations failed to remove that plain and precious teaching. There are too many reliable copies and early quotations out there to hide the evidence as to what the Biblical text actually says.

That's where the not-so-obvious blessing of having so many independent early copies of the Biblical texts kicks in. Nobody was ever in a position of being able to change all of them, without the original reading being preserved somewhere. Remember, Marcion tried to pull off this stunt around 140 AD. He tried to cut everything Jewish out of his New Testament. But he did not succeed in his attempt. We have all the evidence we need that his Bible version was not the original.

Marcion's failure to sell his chop-job on the Bible is why I would argue it is highly unlikely that anyone took out or changed any Bible verses that taught any LDS doctrines, that is, verses that are not found in our present Biblical text. The evidence for such a claim is nowhere to be found.

Neither can we find any evidence that the Bible has been mistranslated at points that are in dispute between Nicene Christians and the LDS church. But translation <u>can</u> make a difference. For example, in Hebrews 7:24, the King James Bible says that the Melchizedek priesthood that Jesus has received is an "unchangeable" priesthood. The Greek term used here, *a-parabaton*, means literally "un-transferable." The LDS church has a Melchizedek priesthood that has been passed to millions of priests. But the Bible actually says that Jesus' priesthood is un-transferable. He is the one and only Melchizedek priest!

So neither text nor translation should be any excuse for faithful Latter-day Saints not to believe the Bible without exception. The same cannot be said when we apply the same questions to the Book of Mormon. Critics have counted 3900 changes between the 1830 version and the version we have today. Again, as in the case of the Bible, the vast majority of these are comparatively minor, such as grammar and spelling. But on what basis are these changes being made: textual, translation, or merely stylistic? We Biblical scholars are content to believe that God has the right to break such human-made rules in cases that do not jeopardize the reader's understanding. So why correct God?

If one believes in the golden plates, then we no longer have access to the original language against which to compare or correct the Book of Mormon's translation. However, if one believes the book to be entirely Joseph's composition, then we have no translation issues in the Book of Mormon, only textual ones. But one change stands out and is worth pondering.

The 1830 version of 2 Nephi 30:6 predicts that the Lamanites (today's Native Americans) would someday become a "white and delightsome people." The handwritten original of this passage confirms these words. But in the church's 1981 edition of the Book of Mormon, this reading was changed to a "pure and delightsome people." Joseph himself tried to make this change in 1840, but later editions chose to follow the original reading.

We have the tools necessary to figure out an accurate text and translation for the Bible, a translation that is accurate enough to meet our needs to know what God wants us to know. For the text of the Hebrew Bible, we have copies of the standard Massoretic text from as early as the 900's AD, a text whose accuracy we can confirm and/or correct by comparison with the Greek translation (200's BCE), the Dead Sea Scrolls (100's BCE – 100 AD), plus ancient evidence from the Aramaic and Latin translations, and the Samaritan Pentateuch. For the New Testament, we have Greek portions in the form of papyrus fragments from as early as 200 AD, complete New Testaments from the 300's AD, plus hundreds of later Greek manuscripts, early translations into Latin, Syriac, and Coptic, plus hundreds of quotes from early Christian writers.

How do we sort through all of this evidence? Scholars have figured out how to weigh which sources are more reliable than others; the earlier and more diverse the sources, the better. We can also look for logical reasons why one reading may be the original and why the change took place. Sometimes we can tell that a letter or word dropped out or was garbled or was confused with another letter or word. Sometimes the shortest reading is best. In cases such as the ending of Mark, the last line of the Lord's Prayer, or the story of the woman caught in adultery in John 8, we must ask: If the longer version was original, why would someone shorten it? And if the shorter version is original, why would someone add to it? Using textual analysis tools like these, we are left with little or no doubt about what God wants us to know.

Likewise, translation is not as mysterious as some might believe. Most of the differences in translation that do not affect the meaning are matters of personal style. Puzzling Hebrew words can often be deciphered from similar words in related languages like Canaanite and Babylonian. A lot can be learned from how a word is used by ancient writers. Did Paul mean "dung" or "garbage" in Philippians 3:8? I demonstrate how to answer that question in one of my "Biblical Words and World" blog posts at Patheos.com, a blog where I have posted nearly forty word studies to show how we can trace the meaning of a Biblical word.

All of this leaves little doubt about what God has said. The real issue is not what God has said, but whether we believe it. Let's apply all of this to the central claim of Joseph: that the true Church ceased to exist after the first century AD.

## A Church That Vanished Without a Trace?

In the *Pearl of Great Price* version of Joseph Smith's First Vision, the gauntlet is thrown down. Joseph is told that he must join none of the churches that exist in his day, because "they were all wrong," and "their creeds were an abomination" in God's sight. In his book *The Great Apostasy*, apostle James Talmage chronicles his case for how the true Church ceased to exist after the first century AD, only to be restored in 1830 by Joseph Smith.[6]

Following the teachings of Joseph, today's LDS church claims that the original Church was led by a living prophet, that the apostles were intended to be an ongoing part of the top leadership, that there was a Melchizedek Priesthood with thousands of male priests, that the majority of the male members ages twelve and up were elders and deacons, that eternal marriages were sealed in their Temple, and that the original church taught the system of doctrine taught in the LDS Church today.

It is the above-described church for which we find no trace in the available hard evidence. As we saw above, in the Biblical description of the Melchizedek priesthood (Hebrews 7:24), we are told that Jesus has an un-transferable (*a-parabaton*) priesthood. Jesus was and is the one and only Melchizedek priest!

There is no prophet leading the Church in the first century AD. There are prophets, such as Agabus (Acts 11:27-28, 21:10), but they are never said to be in leadership, and five of those mentioned are women: Anna (Luke 2:36-38), and the four daughters of Philip (Acts 21:9). In fact, in 2 Kings 22:14, both the priests and King Josiah

---

[6] A stronger case for the Great Apostasy is made by apostle B. H. Roberts in his introduction to Joseph's *History of the Church*. However, Roberts's case is based heavily on the cynical opinions of Edward Gibbons, and on the large number of murders committed by the emperor Constantine. One may ask, Since when does the identity of the true Church depend on the morality of a monarch who did not even belong to that church until late in his life?

must go to the prophetess Huldah for the word of the Lord, and in Judges 4:4-9, General Barak is called to war by the prophetess Deborah.

Biblical prophets do not match the office of prophet in the LDS church. Likewise, the apostles are never said to be a perpetual part of early church leadership, and do not continue into the second century AD. It was never God's plan for them to continue any longer than they did.

Local churches in the first century AD were led by teams who were called "elders" (*presbyteroi*) by the Jews, but were called bishops or literally "overseers" (*episkopoi*) by the Gentiles. In the second century, the *episkopoi* became solo leaders resembling what we call "bishops" today, but nowhere at this time do we find "elders" constituting a majority of the active male membership ages nineteen and up. Nor do deacons appear to have existed in numbers resembling what we find in the Aaronic priesthood of the LDS church (the Aaronic priesthood being another element found nowhere in the true original Church).

The first-century Jewish Temple bears no resemblance to today's LDS temples. We know this because we find blueprints for Solomon's temple in 1 Kings 6, and for Herod's temple in the Mishnah (tractate Middoth). And nowhere in the Bible or rabbinic writings do we find marriage ceremonies of any kind being performed in those temples. Temples were for sacrifice. And now, because of the once-for-all atoning sacrifice of Jesus Christ, temples have become entirely unnecessary (Hebrews 10:11-18).

Furthermore, doctrine does not change in the second century. A robust doctrine of the Trinity, culminating in the Nicene Creed of 325 AD, becomes clearer over time, but simply unpacks what was already there in God's word. Furthermore, there is no LDS doctrine of eternal progression in the early church, a teaching which itself is no logical development, but a stunning innovation from the Trinitarian orthodoxy of the Bible and even the Book of Mormon.

Chains of apostolic succession through the laying on of hands prove nothing. Being able to trace such a chain back to Peter, James, and John (a claim made both by Joseph and by some historic Christian churches) does not prevent church leaders from falling into grave error. The truth that is taught in a particular church is far more reliable evidence of where the true church exists.

Which is the true Church? Nicene Christians (Protestant, Catholic, Orthodox, and all who agree with the Nicene Creed) and Latter-day Saints have tended to agree that both churches can't be true; at least one of them must be false. However, Nicene Christians have tended to de-emphasize the question, while Latter-day Saints have made it central.

The LDS claim to be the true Church fails to prove itself true. The Nicene Church has all the evidence in its favor. One must choose between Joseph's claims and the evidence that we have seen.

# CHAPTER 11

# JOSEPH AS A TRANSLATOR OF SCRIPTURE

One of Joseph's foremost claims as a prophet is his claim to be a translator of God's word. *Doctrine and Covenants* 107:92 states that part of Joseph's job description as head of the church was "to be a seer, a revelator, a translator, and a prophet," gifts that were also to belong to anyone in the future who inherited his position.

## The Book of Mormon: No Original to Cross-Check

We have no original text against which to test Joseph's claim to have translated the Book of Mormon, but we can examine his attempts to retranslate the Bible, and his claim to have translated the words of Abraham in Egypt, a translation found in the LDS scriptural volume *Pearl of Great Price.* Can Joseph translate, as he claims that he could and did?

To determine whether Joseph's golden plates actually existed, as the famous groups of three witnesses and eight witnesses testify, is beyond the capacity of the historian to tell. So too is the existence of a text on those plates in an otherwise unknown language, as we are told this was. The question is whether one views the Book of Mormon as a nineteenth century composition, or a translation of an ancient document. If it is a translation, it was not done by linguistic methods, but rather by what amounts to direct revelation, and thus becomes a matter as to whether we can trust Joseph to reveal to us a book that professes to be from God.

Could an uneducated man like Joseph have composed the Book of Mormon, with or without the sources that he is claimed to have plagiarized? It is claimed that Joseph actually composed the book borrowing heavily from Ethan Smith's *View of the Hebrews,* and/or from an unpublished frontier novel written by Solomon Spaulding, and may even have had the help of Sidney Rigdon, a pastor in Alexander Campbell's restorationist movement who soon became one of Joseph's followers and a key leader in the early LDS church.

However, writing from the perspective of critical historians, both Fawn Brodie and Richard Bushman doubt these theories.[1] They give Joseph credit for producing the book without the help of any contemporary sources, other than what appear to be lengthy borrowings from the King James Version of the Bible. They, along with others, observe how much the book reflects the time, culture, and language of Joseph's day, more so than that of ancient Mesoamerica.

Bushman gives us a stimulating discussion of the Book of Mormon unlike any that I have seen. He expresses wonder at how Joseph could have produced such a text: "During the three months of rapid translation, Joseph

---

[1] Brodie, *No Man Knows My History,* 67-73; Bushman, *Rough Stone Rolling,* 84-108.

seemed to be in the grip of creative forces beyond himself, the pages pouring from his mind like *Messiah* from the pen of Handel." Bushman cites Emma Smith, who tells that Joseph would dictate to her hour after hour, then leave, and then pick up exactly where he left off.[2]

Whether the Book of Mormon's contents are true, is a different issue than the issues of translation or composition. Bushman makes persuasive cases for both sides as to whether the book's content is true or false. He acknowledges DNA research that connects Native Americans (the main characters of the Book of Mormon) to east Asian rather than to Semitic origins. He briefly gives both sides of the archaeological debate.

There are admitted difficulties in doing Book of Mormon archaeology, because there is so little written language material available from the area in question. Therefore, it is virtually impossible to identify cities or areas such as Bountiful or Zarahemla. Horses and donkeys (Ether 9:19), elephants (Ether 9:19), oxen and pigs (Ether 9:18), silk (Alma 1:29), and wheat (Mosiah 9:9), all items that are mentioned in the Book of Mormon as having existed in ancient America, remain unconfirmed by archaeology.

I have no problem with the idea that Jesus may have visited America, as the Book of Mormon states; it would correlate with today's appearances of Jesus in the dreams of Muslims, and would fit the white god traditions of Central and South America and the South Pacific. But if Jesus did come to America, this does not mean that the Book of Mormon's account thereof is true. The migration of Jews to America in 600 BC is much harder to support. Even harder to defend is the passage in 3 Nephi 8:5-25 where, before the arrival of Jesus, cities fall and are buried or sink into the sea, accompanied by earthquakes and storms, and three days of darkness.

But some, like Bushman, do not need the Book of Mormon to be factually true to still be a revelation from God. One can find truth in works of fiction such as Orwell's *1984* or *Star Wars*. The question is whether this would fit what Joseph intended us to believe.

To me, the Book of Mormon reads like a product of the theology of the 1820's. It is an impressive product indeed, reflecting both the rough education and the sharp mind of its author, able to retain and synthesize the preaching and religious literature of his day into a sizeable volume of work. I will give Joseph Smith credit for a masterful creation, but I would argue that the only parts of it that are inspired by God are the parts that are restatements of Biblical truth.

## The Bible: Joseph's Word against the Available Evidence

In our previous chapter, in the context of Article 8's claim to believe the Bible "as far as it is translated correctly," we discussed the issue of whether the Bible's text and translation is accurate. In practice, the Latter-day Saints have resolved the issue for themselves in two contrasting ways.

The first way to deal with a Biblical text that could not be entirely trusted is that Joseph made his own translation of the Bible, which has been published by the Reorganized LDS church.[3] Joseph used the King James translation for his version, but made alterations as he was so inclined. (See http://www.mormonthink.com/jst.htm.)

It is been observed that at some points, Joseph's Bible contradicts places where the same Bible passages are quoted verbatim in the Book of Mormon. An example is Matthew 7:6 = 3 Nephi 14:6, which is translated by Joseph as follows (added words are in italics): "*And the mysteries of the kingdom ye shall keep within yourselves; for it is not meet to* give ~~not~~ that which is holy unto the dogs; neither cast ye your pearls unto swine, lest they trample them

[2] Bushman, *Rough Stone Rolling*, 105.

[3] Joseph Smith, Jr., *The Holy Scriptures – Inspired Version* (Independence: Herald Publishing House, 1991).

under their feet. *For the world cannot receive that which ye, yourselves, are not able to bear; wherefore ye shall not give your pearls unto them, lest they* ~~and~~ *turn again and rend you.*"

It has also been observed that there are dozens of Bible verses that have been determined to be late scribal additions, or contain scribal alterations, verses that Joseph included without alteration in his translation. The clearest example is 1 John 5:7-8, where a reference to the Trinity that is found only in four late medieval Greek manuscripts is included in the King James Version. The words "in heaven, the Father, the Word, and the Holy Ghost, and these three are one. And there are three that bear witness on earth" are never quoted by ancient Greek theologians, only by Latin theologians from the fifth century onward, nor are they found in any of the ancient translations such as Syriac, Coptic, or Armenian. Yet Joseph includes these words in his *Inspired Version*, although most LDS scholars agree that they are late additions to the text.

Joseph mistranslates Golgotha as "burial" rather than "skull," and translates Cephas as either "a seer or a stone" (John 1:42). Joseph sometimes adds details in his translation with no apparent explanation or apologetic value. He alters Genesis 8:21 to say it was Noah and not God who smelled the pleasing odor from his sacrifice after the Flood. He also fails to correct verses in the Bible that contradict his later teachings on eternal marriage and on the plurality of gods; if Joseph had the truth, why did he not correct these Biblical texts accordingly?

One very important addition that Joseph makes in his translation is in Genesis 50:24, where he adds 13 verses (over 800 words), including a prediction that God will send a "choice seer," that he will write words for the "confounding of false doctrines... And that seer I will bless...and his name shall be called Joseph, and it shall be after the name of his father..." Joseph's addition is found neither in our oldest complete Hebrew manuscripts (tenth century AD), nor are they found in the Greek Septuagint (275 BC), nor in the Dead Sea Scrolls (150 BC – 70 AD), nor in the Samaritan Pentateuch (pre-Christian period). Clearly this prediction would have been "plain and precious" if it had been part of the original text, but the evidence that it was ever part of the original text is non-existent.

Another addition by Joseph for which we have no Greek (or any other) manuscript evidence is inserted between our Matthew 9:15 and 9:16, where the Inspired Version reads, "Then said the Pharisees unto him, Why will ye not receive us with our baptism, seeing we keep the whole law? But Jesus said unto them, Ye keep not the law. If ye had kept the law, ye would have received me; for I am he who gave the law. I receive not you with your baptism because it profiteth you nothing. For when that which is new is come, the old is ready to be put away."

Extended examples of Joseph's alterations in his translations may be seen in his retranslations of the Genesis creation in the Book of Moses and the Book of Abraham. Since Joseph does not claim to have access to original Biblical manuscripts, it would appear that he is relying on what he believes to be direct revelation for his translation.

For instance, Joseph tells one audience, "Many things in the Bible which do not, as they now stand, accord with the revelation of the Holy Ghost to me. Ponder "This day thou sha[l]t be with me in paradise." Paradise, [a] Modern word, don't answer to the original word used by Jesus."[4] Joseph tells another audience, "I believe the Bible, as it ought to be, as it came from the pen of the original writers. As it read[s] it repented the Lord that he had made man. And also, God is not a man that he should repent, which I do not believe. But it repented Noah that God made man. This I believe and then the other quotation stands fair."[5] Again, there is zero textual evidence for either of these proposed changes by Joseph.

The main branch of the LDS church, rather than using Joseph's translation, simply defers to the King James Bible, and usually appeals to their additional scriptures on issues where the Bible disagrees with them, where they

---

[4] Diary of Joseph Smith, June 11, 1843, in *American Prophet's Record*, 384.

[5] Diary of Joseph Smith, October 15, 1843, in *American Prophet's Record*, 420.

can cite their eighth Article of Faith. However, the LDS church has also published a study Bible with copious foot-notes from the Joseph Smith translation wherever his translation differs from the King James Version.

## Joseph's Knowledge of Hebrew

Joseph and some of his leaders did have a few Hebrew lessons from a Jew named Joshua Seixas. Joseph is cor-rect when he names his city of Nauvoo after the Hebrew word "beautiful" (*nawū'*). His use of the words *gnolaum* (Abraham 3:18) and *Raukeeyang* in the *Pearl of Great Price* have puzzled scholars, but they actually are the words "eternal" (*'olam*) and "firmament" (*raqia'*), with the letter *'ayin* pronounced as an "ng" instead of silent, while *Hah-Ko-kau-beam* and *Shaumahyeem* are good Hebrew for "the stars" (*ha-kokabīm*) and "heavens" (*shamayim*).

A classic example of how Joseph translated Hebrew is found in his famous sermon on eternal progression and the plurality of gods on April 7, 1844:

"I shall comment on the very first Hebrew word in the Bible; I will make a comment on the very first sentence of the history of creation in the Bible – *Berosheit.* I want to analyze the word. *Baith* – in, by, through, and everything else. *Rosh* – the head, *Sheit* – grammatical termination. When the inspired man wrote it, he did not put the baith there. An old Jew without any authority added the word; he thought it too bad to begin to talk about the head! It read first, 'The head one of the Gods brought forth the Gods.' That is the true meaning of the words. *Baurau* signi-fies to bring forth. If you do not believe it, you do not believe the learned man of God. Learned men can teach you no more than what I have told you. Thus the head God brought forth the Gods in the grand council." (*Journal of Discourses* 6:4-5)

Here is a huge example of a place where even Joseph's *Inspired Version* fails to render the text the way Joseph translates the passage in this sermon. Here Joseph actually uses a few bits of Hebrew, although his understanding is garbled. Notice that Joseph makes *Elohim* (which he translates "god<u>s</u>" rather than "God") the object of the verb, while he ignores "heaven and earth," which <u>are</u> marked as objects of the verb by the Hebrew particle -*eth*. Joseph also translates the verb *bara'* as "brought forth" rather than "created (out of nothing)."

Later in the same sermon, Joseph says, "It does not say in the Hebrew that God created the spirit of man. It says, 'God made man out of the earth, and put into him Adam's spirit, and so became a living body.'" (*Journal of Discourses* 6:6) Here he is playing with the double use of *adam* as the noun "man" and the name Adam, although he is also adding to and twisting the text.

## The Book of Abraham: No Resemblance to the Text

Aside from Joseph's revisions of the Bible, for which there were no original manuscripts to which to appeal, no one had been able to test Joseph's ability to translate. That is, until 1967, when there came some shocking news, delivered by BYU professor Hugh Nibley, one of the top defenders of the LDS Church:

"The papyri scripts given to the Church do not prove the Book of Abraham is true." Dr. Nibley goes on to warn his audience, "LDS scholars are caught flat footed by this discovery." There it was, on page four of BYU's *Daily Universe* on Friday, December 1, 1967. (Good luck finding a photocopy! You won't find it online. It is old news that has been "shadow-banned" for decades.)

To an academic assembly at BYU, Nibley inadvertently confesses that a document which they had hoped would prove Joseph Smith's ability to translate ancient scripture had just been found to be anything but proof. Nibley goes on to express to his audience his fear that discoveries like this were going to "bury the Church in criticism."

The discovery to which Nibley refers was an Egyptian papyri text from which Joseph translated the Book of Abraham in the *Pearl of Great Price*. Joseph's source was found on a mummy that he bought from a traveling salesman. Joseph declared that he had found the words of Abraham written while he was in Egypt, which Joseph proceeded to translate. At the same time, Joseph composed his *Egyptian Alphabet and Grammar*, in which he demonstrates how he translated the text.[6]

It was thought that the Book of Abraham papyri had been lost. But then they reappeared in 1967 at the Metropolitan Museum of Art in New York, from which the LDS church obtained them. Now, Joseph's translation could be tested. The results could help confirm Joseph's ability to translate the Book of Mormon as well, although no one possesses the golden plates which Joseph claims to have translated.

The results proved to be an embarrassment. The text turned out to be a pagan Egyptian funeral text from approximately the first century AD, almost 2000 years after Abraham. Several scholars, both LDS and secular, made translations that agreed with one another. These translations reveal that for every one Egyptian word in the text, Joseph used anywhere from fifty to over 150 words in his translation, including 178 words for the name of the Egyptian deity Khons (the entirety of Abraham 1:16-19).

The eleven pages of the Book of Abraham (approximately 5470 words) are "translated" from the following Egyptian words: "...the great pool of Khonsu [Osirus Hor, justified], born of Taykhebet, a man likewise. After (his) two arms are [fas]tened to his breast, one wraps the Book of Breathings, which is with writing both inside and outside of it, with royal linen, it being placed at (his) left arm near his heart, this having been done at his wrapping and outside it. If this book be recited for him, then he will breath like the soul[s of the gods] for ever and ever."[7]

In his own translation of the Egyptian text, Nibley himself could not evade the truth about what the papyri text actually said. So he spent years of his life and work trying to find an alternative way to understand the Book of Abraham and its connection (or lack thereof) to the text that Joseph had claimed to have translated. He eventually published his conclusions in his book *The Joseph Smith Papyri: An Egyptian Endowment*.

Nibley's basic theory was that Joseph's book was actually not a translation, but an imaginative expansion on the meaning of his text, comparable to the Jewish *midrashim* or "commentaries" on the Hebrew Bible. (My explanation here is itself a *midrash* on what Nibley actually said. Nibley never used the term *midrash*.) Other LDS scholars have suggested that Joseph used the Egyptian text as a "super-cryptogram" or a memory device. These theories are refuted by Joseph himself in his handwritten manuscript included in his *Egyptian Alphabet and Grammar*, where he says it is "A Translation of the Book of Abraham written by his own hand upon papyrus and found in the catacombs of Egypt." (See the similar preface in the printed version of the *Pearl of Great Price*.)

If I were diehard LDS, I would probably resort to Nibley's redefinition of the word "translation." But for me, and for anyone who is more committed to the honest truth than to any ideology, the truth about the Book of Abraham would be like (theoretically) digging up the bones of Jesus: proof that Joseph did not have the faintest idea what he was translating, and indirect proof that none of his translations were from God, including the Book of Mormon.

For me, here is solid proof that Joseph was a deceiver, a false prophet. The truth about the Book of Abraham is a major piece of what keeps me from being won over by the attractiveness of the LDS church.

I have spent forty-one years studying the LDS people and their story. I find them fascinating, and I have a great burden in my heart for them to know the truth, both about Joseph, and about Jesus. If any LDS person asks me the

---

[6] Text obtainable at http://www.utlm.org/booklist/titles/josephsmithegyptianpapers_ub010.htm.

[7] John A. Wilson, Richard A. Parker, et al., "The Joseph Smith Egyptian Papyri," *Dialogue: A Journal of Mormon Thought* 3, no. 2 (Summer 1968): 98. Download the entire issue at https://www.dialoguejournal.com/wp-content/uploads/sbi/issues/V03N02.pdf.

Golden Question, "Why haven't you become one of us?", the evidence on the Book of Abraham would be part of my answer.

But I have no desire to take away any Latter-day Saint's faith in all that they hold sacred. My desire is for them to transfer all of their faith onto Jesus instead of Joseph. Jesus is the truth who will never let you down. You were never wrong to place your faith in him! The bedrock truth of Jesus' resurrection endures when all other claims of faith on the market collapse. And faith in his saving death on the cross is the only way you can know for sure that you have been saved from your sins and eternally put right with God.

# CHAPTER 12

# DID JOSEPH DIE A MARTYR'S DEATH?

## Joseph Declared a Martyr

The way the story is often told, Joseph Smith died as a martyr to his faith. In *Journal of Discourses* 7:289, Brigham Young declares that Joseph "was a martyr to his religion and to the name of Christ." In *Journal of Discourses* 3:48, again Brigham says, "It is impossible for a Prophet of Christ to live in an adulterous generation without speaking of the wickedness of the people, without revealing their faults and their failings, and there is nothing short of death that will stay him from it… It was for this that they killed Joseph and Hyrum, it is for this that they wish to kill me and my brethren…"

After its official narrative describing the death of Joseph and his brother Hyrum, the LDS scripture *Doctrine and Covenants* declares in Section 135: "[Joseph] lived great, and he died great in the eyes of God and his people; and like most of the Lord's anointed in ancient times, has sealed his mission and his works with his own blood…" (135:3)

Section 135 goes on to say that the names of Joseph and his brother Hyrum "will be classed among the martyrs of religion; and the reader in every nation will be reminded that the Book of Mormon, and this book of Doctrine and Covenants of the church, cost the best blood of the nineteenth century… They lived for glory; they died for glory; and glory is their eternal reward. From age to age shall their names go down to posterity as gems for the sanctified. They were innocent of any crime…and their *innocent blood*, with the innocent blood of all the martyrs under the altar that John saw, will cry unto the Lord of Hosts till he avenges that blood on earth." (135:6-7, emphasis original)

In the final section of *Doctrine and Covenants*, where Brigham Young gives orders for the migration to the West as "the word and will of the Lord," Brigham declares: "Many have marveled because of his death; but it was needful that he should seal his testimony with his blood that he might be honored and the wicked might be condemned." (136:39)

When surrendering himself to prison for the last time, Joseph reportedly said, "I am going like a lamb to the slaughter…**I shall die innocent**" (135:4, emphasis original).

Did Joseph die defending the truth of what he preached? Or did he end up in the prison where he was lynched, for the crime of destroying an opponent's printing press to cover up his practice of plural marriage?

## The Specifics of What Happened That Day

The *Nauvoo Expositor* published its one and only issue on June 7, 1844.[1] One finds immediately that the publishers are by no means anti-Mormon, since they are upfront about their belief in the Book of Mormon and the "Book of Covenants." However, they firmly believe that Joseph is a sexually immoral deceiver and a dangerous political despot. Their claims about Joseph's practice of plural marriage are backed up in detail by the evidence we saw in chapter 7. They further allege on page five that Joseph has been preaching "other Gods above the God of this creation," that he has been involved in a real estate racket, and that he has set himself up as king and lawgiver for the church. Some in Nauvoo feared the *Expositor* because they believed that its claims were false; Joseph and his leaders must have feared it because they knew how much of it was true.

The account in *History of the Church* 6:441 quotes the minutes of the Nauvoo City Council, which quote the Mayor (Joseph Smith) as saying that "if he had a City Council who felt as he did, the [*Nauvoo Expositor*] would be declared a nuisance before night…" City Council member Hyrum Smith is quoted as saying that the best way to deal with it was "to smash the press and pi the type" (*History of the Church* 6:445). The result, in Joseph's words: "The Council passed an ordinance declaring the Nauvoo Expositor a nuisance, and also issued an order to me to abate the said nuisance. I immediately ordered the Marshal to destroy it without delay" (*History of the Church* 6:432). The evidence indicates that Joseph was directly responsible for what was done, albeit through his City Council. One wonders whether Joseph would have ordered that printing press destroyed, if he had known that it would lead to his death.

If Joseph had not been murdered by the mob, he likely would have been convicted of polygamy, for which he says a local grand jury indicted him less than a month before his death.[2] Joseph says he was jailed on a charge of treason (*History of the Church* 6:562, 613), but it is unlikely that the particulars of his case would have resulted in a death penalty, although the rumor was circulating that Joseph had been anointed king in Nauvoo,[3] which no doubt contributed to the ferocity of the mob arrayed against him.

Contrary to the way the story is often told, Joseph did not die peacefully, according to faithful Latter-day Saints on the scene, but successfully defended himself with a six-shooter smuggled into the jail. Apostle (later Prophet) John Taylor tells us, "Elder Cyrus H. Wheelock came in to see us, and when he was about leaving drew a small pistol, a six-shooter, from his pocket, remarking at the same time, 'Would any of you like to have this?' Brother Joseph immediately replied, 'Yes, give it to me,' whereupon he took the pistol, and put it in his pantaloons pocket." (*History of the Church* 7:100)

It appears to be Willard Richards, Joseph's personal scribe, who was in the prison cell with Joseph, who narrates the version of the story in volume 6 of *History of the Church*: "Joseph sprang to his coat for his six-shooter, Hyrum for his single barrel" (*History of the Church* 6:617). "When Hyrum fell, Joseph exclaimed, 'Oh dear, brother Hyrum!' and opening the door a few inches he discharged his six shooter in the stairway (as stated before), two or three barrels of which missed fire… Joseph, seeing there was no safety in the room, and no doubt thinking that it would save the lives of his brethren in the room if he could get out, turned calmly from the door, dropped his pistol on the floor and sprang into the window when two balls pierced him from the door, and one entered his right breast

---

[1] Full text available at both www.fairmormon.org and www.mormonism.net (PDF).

[2] Diary of Joseph Smith, May 25, 1844, in *American Prophet's Record*, 483.

[3] See the discussion of Joseph's anointing as king by the Council of Fifty in Bushman, *Rough Stone Rolling*, 519-525.

from without, and he fell outward into the hands of his murderers, exclaiming, 'O Lord, my God!'" (*History of the Church* 6:618)

"When the jail in Carthage was assailed, and the mob was pouring murderous volleys into the room occupied by himself and friends, the Prophet turned from the prostrate form of his murdered brother to face death-dealing guns and bravely returned the fire of his assailants, 'bringing his man down every time,' and compelling even John Hay, who but reluctantly accords the Prophet any quality of virtue, to confess that he 'made a handsome fight' in the jail." (*History of the Church* 6: xli)

The Introduction to volume 6 of *History of the Church* offers the following footnote to the above passage: "This is the late Secretary of State John Hay, in the *Atlantic Monthly* for December, 1869; 'Joe Smith died bravely, he stood by the jam of the door and fired four shots, bringing his man down every time. He shot an Irishman named Wills, who was in the affair from his congenital love of a brawl, in the arm; Gallaghor, a Southerner from the Mississippi bottom, in the face; Voorhees, a half-grown hobbledehoy from Bear Creek, in the shoulder; and another gentleman, whose name I will not mention, as he in prepared to prove an *alibi*, and besides stands six feet two in his moccasins.' In a later paragraph he refers to 'the handsome fight in the jail.'" (*History of the Church* 6: xli, fn27)

John Taylor, third Prophet of the LDS Church, tells it this way: "I shall never forget the deep feeling of sympathy and regard manifested in the countenance of Brother Joseph as he drew nigh to Hyrum, and, leaning over him, exclaimed, 'Oh! my poor, dear brother Hyrum!' He, however, instantly arose, and with a firm, quick step, and a determined expression of countenance, approached the door, and pulling the six-shooter left by Brother Wheelock from his pocket, opened the door slightly, and snapped the pistol six successive times; only three of the barrels, however, were discharged. I afterwards understood that two or three were wounded by these discharges, two of whom, I am informed, died." (*History of the Church* 7:102)

According to the same LDS sources, Joseph requests a pipe and tobacco for Willard Richards: "Dr. Richards was taken sick, when Joseph said, 'Brother Markham, as you have a pass from the Governor to go in and out of the jail, go and get the doctor a pipe and some tobacco to settle his stomach,' and Markham went he had got the pipe and tobacco." (*History of the Church* 6:614)

Joseph also sends for wine that day: "Before the jailor came in, his boy brought in some water, and said the guard wanted some wine. Joseph gave Dr. Richards two dollars to give the guard; but the guard said one was enough, and would take no more. The guard immediately sent for a bottle of wine, pipes, and two small papers of tobacco; and one of the guards brought them into the jail soon after the jailor went out. Dr. Richards uncorked the bottle, and presented a glass to Joseph, who tasted, as also Brother Taylor and the doctor, and the bottle was then given to the guard, who turned to go out." (6:616)

Apostle (later Prophet) John Taylor adds details: "Sometime after dinner we sent for some wine. **It has been reported by some that this was taken as a sacrament. It was no such thing; our spirits were generally dull and heavy, and it was sent for to revive us...** I believe we all drank of the wine, and gave some to one or two of the prison guards. We all of us felt unusually dull and languid, with a remarkable depression of spirits. In consonance with those feelings I sang a song, that had lately been introduced into Nauvoo, entitled, 'A Poor Wayfaring Man of Grief', etc." (*History of the Church* 7:101, emphasis added)

Do these accounts sound at odds with the traditional telling of Joseph's death? They all come to us from the official *History of the Church*, originally edited after Joseph's death by Brigham Young, John Taylor, George A. Smith, and Heber Kimball, the most loyal followers of Joseph we can find.[4] We have the word of the first three prophets

---

[4] Brigham's first reference to "revising" or editing Joseph's history is found in *History of the Church* 7:389, followed by fifteen further references to "revising" in volume 7, naming those who helped him on each occasion.

of the LDS church, plus Joseph's personal scribe, none of whom appears to have any motive to lie about these details of what happened. Both the criteria of embarrassment and multiple sources apply. What is troubling is how often the story is "sanitized" to give a misleading impression of the way that Joseph died.[5]

## Unjustified Homicide, or Martyrdom?

There was, and is, no justification for Joseph's death. Neither polygamy nor adultery, nor the destruction of property for which he was imprisoned at the last, carried a death penalty anywhere in the United States. None of the political or religious reasons why the Latter-day Saints were hated were valid reasons for the killings done by the Carthage mob.

But as tragic and senseless as their deaths were, this does not mean that the deaths of Joseph and Hyrum Smith can properly be considered martyrdom. Although he was most definitely the victim of the worst violent injustice, Joseph did not die innocent. He died either covering up a crime, or (if one chooses to see it this way) covering up a principle of faith. If he had confessed the truth about what he was doing, he might not have died this way. And if he had died for confessing the truth, then he could have been properly considered a martyr.

Joseph did not die for saying, "Plural marriage is from God; I will die defending it." Nor did he die for refusing to deny the Book of Mormon or his teachings. He does not die for reasons comparable to the martyrdoms of early Christians who refused to worship Caesar.

Compare the death of Joseph to the death of Jesus. Jesus refused to let Peter defend him with the sword (Matthew 26:52). And Jesus dies innocent of sin (1 Peter 2:22, 2 Corinthians 5:21). He was innocent of political charges: three times Pilate declares, "I find no crime in him." (Luke 23:3-22) He was guilty only of answering "I am" to the question, "Are you the Messiah, the Son of the Blessed One?" at his Jewish trial. (Mark 14:61-62*)

Yes, both Jesus and Joseph die because those who were in power hated and feared them. Both surrendered to their enemies when they easily could have evaded capture. But here the resemblances end.

Does the question of martyrdom make a difference in our verdict on Joseph? Even if we decide that his death does not exactly fit our definition of martyrdom, the basic picture of Joseph's character and trustworthiness remains pretty much unchanged. The fact that he was killed because he was hated is despicable, but it was not inevitable; he is the lone nineteenth-century religious leader to be lynched out of pure animosity. Such a death is also not the same as if he died as a direct result of what his faith required him to believe or do.

The evidence shows us that Joseph was killed for an act of suppressing the truth about either his immorality or his faith. It is meritorious to die for affirming one's faith, but not for hiding it, or for covering up one's sin.

---

[5] To its credit, the recent official LDS biography *Saints: The Standard of Truth* does affirm the gunfight, but it still titles the chapter about Joseph's death "A Lamb to the Slaughter," and fails to mention the wine and tobacco.

# CHAPTER 13

# BY THEIR FRUITS SHALL WE KNOW THEM?

### How Can Falsehood Produce So Much Good?

If we conclude that Joseph was not a prophet of God, or that he was in fact a deceiver, then how do we explain all the good we see in the church that considers him to be their quintessential prophet? As the LDS church eagerly argues, in the words of Jesus, "You will know them by their fruits." Can a prophet who appears to be false, end up starting a church that proves to be the real deal (if not the only one)?

How can a church be false, when its people do so much good? Can God be at work within what might appear to be a false church? If the historic Christian church that holds to the Nicene Creed proves to be the true Church, can a person come to a saving knowledge of Jesus Christ as a member of the wrong church, or will they be automatically lost? Does following a false prophet send you to hell?

I grappled with these questions while visiting a local LDS stake conference meeting in a small town in central Utah. The guest speaker was a member of the First Quorum of Seventy. I saw and heard powerful conversion stories and testimonies of changed lives. How could I explain all this?

Several scriptures come to mind. In Mark 9:38-39*, John says to Jesus, "Teacher, we saw someone casting out demons in your name, and we tried to stop him, because he was not following us. But Jesus said, Do not stop him, for no one who does a deed of power in my name will be able soon afterward to speak evil of me."

In Philippians 1:15-18, Paul reacts to the fact that while he is in prison, the Christian message is spreading out of control. While some who are preaching Christ are fully on board with Paul and his Gospel, some are preaching Christ out of rivalry, seeking to defeat Paul in the race to reach human souls. They're preaching a Jesus that requires people to obey the Jewish law to be saved.

But what is Paul's reaction? "What, then (shall I say)? Only that in every way, whether in pretense or in truth, Christ is proclaimed, and in this I rejoice." (Philippians 1:18*) The apostle Paul is thrilled that Jesus is being proclaimed, even by legalists in his day, because God can use the name of Jesus to lead people to salvation from sin, even in a movement where people are trying mistakenly to save themselves by their own good works.

So how do we explain what God appears to be doing in a church that rejects historic Christianity? The answer may be that many people in the LDS church are finding the Jesus of historic Christianity, despite the LDS church's official rejection thereof. People there are thirsty for Jesus and his living water, and Jesus is meeting that powerful thirst, even though they are swallowing what I believe are a lot of toxic elements mixed with that living water.

Much of the vitality in the LDS Church is inspired by a message of salvation through Christ's atonement that is not LDS, but evangelical Christian. Many LDS have a faith that is more evangelical Christian than it is LDS. Glenn Beck's theology sounds more like Billy Graham than Joseph Smith. I see this phenomenon as the reason why numerous LDS may find themselves being saved from Joseph's eternal fate, and why God seems to be producing the fruits of the Spirit in such people.

It is worth noting that the high sexual morality that has been courageously defended by today's LDS church was not gotten from the personal example of Joseph Smith, but actually contradicts his example. This is what Jesus really means when he says, "You will know them by their fruits." We know a church, not by the fruits of their followers, but by the fruits of the prophet they follow.

A comparison with Islam is helpful. Should Muhammad be judged by the deeds of his people, or by his own teachings and example? A huge number of today's Muslims are peaceful, generous people who have done a world of good. But are these fruits directly traceable to their prophet, or to their own innate character, or to teachings borrowed from the Judeo-Christian tradition? How did the prophet Muhammad actually live (according to his own words and the words of those who followed him), and what did he really say?

The fruits of Jesus work the same way. While Christians have been widely criticized for violence such as the Crusades, such evils only happen when Christians are not following the teachings and example of Jesus. For an exploration of whether today's terrorists are following or disobeying Muhammad, I refer you to my article, "Jesus and Muhammad."[1]

In recent years, the LDS church has been putting a strong emphasis on Christ's atonement. As they do so, they have been messaging a different doctrine of atonement than what they themselves have always taught. The LDS talk a lot about the Savior, but they are unclear on the question "Savior from what?" The LDS Articles of Faith teach that Jesus saves us only from the effects of Adam's sin, so that now people can be saved by obedience to the laws and ordinances of their gospel. The LDS have also tended to deemphasize the cross, as we see from the absence of crosses anywhere on their buildings. (A surprising exception that contradicts the rule: Alma 34:10-15 proclaims a doctrine of the Atonement that reads like it was written by St. Anselm!)

So the recent effort to proclaim the historic Christian version of Jesus taking away all of our sin is not very LDS at all, but it does speak to the hearts of multitudes who are desperate to know God's forgiveness. Sadly, what newcomers get after they join the LDS church is a works-based theology that is a burden to the soul. That's why my heart went out to the LDS when I first met them. Grace is almost nowhere to be found. Life becomes an endless treadmill of obedience and obligation that drives many to depression. And how can we deal with our need for forgiveness when we fail?

The LDS prophet Spencer Kimball describes forgiveness in his book *The Miracle of Forgiveness* as such a long process of suffering, contrition, and penitence that it sounds like a miracle if anyone ever obtains it. He says, "Your Heavenly Father has promised forgiveness upon total repentance and meeting all the requirements, but that forgiveness is not granted merely for the asking. There must be works – many works – and an all-out, total surrender, with a great humility and 'a broken heart and contrite spirit.' It depends upon you whether or not you are forgiven, and when. It could be weeks, it could be years, it could be centuries before that happy day when you have positive assurance that the Lord has forgiven you. That depends on your humility, your sincerity, your works."[2]

In the official LDS church manual *Gospel Principles*, Kimball is quoted as saying, "There is no royal road to

---

[1] Tom Hobson, "Jesus and Muhammad," *Presbyterian Outlook*, online: https://pres-outlook.org/2010/09/jesus-and-muhammad/, accessed 2/13/2019.

[2] Spencer Kimball, *The Miracle of Forgiveness* (Salt Lake City: Bookcraft, 1969), 324-325.

repentance, no privileged path to forgiveness... There is only one way. It is a long road spiked with thorns and briars and pitfalls and problems."[3] Is this the Good News of the Gospel that inspires people to enthusiastically follow? Does this burden naturally follow from the teachings of Joseph?

2 Nephi 25:23 speaks of grace, then pulls the rug out from under the principle when it says, "For we know that it is by grace that we are saved, after all we can do." Similarly, Mosiah 4:29-30 says, "I cannot tell you all the things whereby ye may commit sin; for there are divers ways and means, even so many that I cannot number them. But this much I can tell you, that if you do not watch yourselves, and your thoughts, and your words, and your deeds, and observe the commandments of God, and continue in the faith of what ye have heard concerning the coming of our Lord, even unto the end of your lives, ye must perish."

## Can God Use Falsehood to Lead People to the Truth?

As we have seen in chapter 9, even if Jesus is working within the LDS church to draw people to himself, he is doing so within a church with a very different understanding of God. Can God work within a church with such a false view of God? Apparently so. One suspects that God similarly chose to save people inside the ancient Gnostic and Arian heresies. We know that God used the Nestorians, who had a Doctor Jekyll/Mister Hyde doctrine of Jesus, as the first missionaries to China. We know that God used the Arians, who denied that Jesus was God, to reach the Goths with the message of Jesus. But that's no reason for us not to reach out to those who are entangled in serious deception.

God uses people I'd never think of using. God uses a violent sex addict named Samson to save Israel from their enemies. God uses a pagan king, Cyrus of Persia, to set his people free from Babylon, and even calls Cyrus "my anointed one" ("*Messiah*" – Isaiah 45:1). God uses what he's got, and doesn't always wait for us to get our act together. God uses adulterous leaders to bring souls to Christ, while faithful pastors often labor for years without visible results. God even uses false teaching to make us do our homework, so that we can do a better job proclaiming the truth. God judges the sin and false teaching of church leaders on his own timetable, and it may not be clear until later what God is doing. But that doesn't mean that God doesn't care about truth or righteousness, or that it's not important for us to reject and correct falsehood and sin.

The danger is that if one follows a false prophet, one may end up going where that prophet goes. Jesus says, "Many will say to me in that day, Lord, Lord, did we not prophesy in your name, and cast out demons in your name, and do many powerful deeds in your name? And then I will confess to them: I never knew you." (Matthew 7:22-23*) If you follow a false prophet, you are in danger of ending up where the false prophet leads you. You are not guaranteed to be lost, but we need to take Jesus' warning in Matthew 7 with the utmost seriousness.

I would argue that, as is the case with Islam, anything good in the LDS church actually comes from the Bible as its source. In neither Islam nor the LDS church does the new prophet bring a major or unique teaching that improves on the Biblical message. Therefore, any appeals to Jesus' words "You will know them by their fruits" may be answered by saying that what we are seeing are the fruits of doctrine rather than the fruits that indicate whether a prophet truly comes from God. To the extent that New Testament doctrine is faithfully lived out, we should expect good fruit, even if it is practiced by followers who believe substantial amounts of false doctrine mixed into their message. But if there is false doctrine in our church, we should still seek to either correct that doctrine or avoid it.

Plenty of people seriously consider leaving the historic Christian Church because of all the garbage going on in it. Plenty of LDS think of leaving their church for the same reason. That desire is easy to understand, but we

[3] Church of Jesus Christ of Latter-day Saints, *Gospel Principles* (Salt Lake City: Corporation of the President, 1979), 118.

should not be surprised by the garbage we find in either place. In fact, to find evil in the visible earthly church is exactly what Biblical doctrine leads us to expect: "The heart is deceitful above all things, and hopelessly sick. Who can understand it?" (Jeremiah 17:9*) Whichever place is the true Church, the Church is a hospital for recovering sinners; we shouldn't be surprised if it's full of staph and MRSA, figuratively speaking.

Yes, there are times when even the true Church hardly resembles the Bride of Christ. But it proves nothing if we hold a contest to see which church is on its best behavior. It proves nothing if we try to quantify how much good or evil has been done by the historic Christian Church, or how much good or evil has been done by followers of Joseph. Although our behavior can be bad advertising for our faith, the truth of God's Church does not depend on the goodness of her members. I believe the resurrection of Jesus was true, even if every follower of his proves to be a jerk.

## Can Both Churches Be True?

Can Jesus be at work in the LDS church? Jesus did not object when a guy who did not follow him used his name to cast out demons (although in Acts 19:13-16, demons themselves challenge a similar exorcist's right to do so). But in every possible instance where God seems to be at work in the LDS church, we must ask: Is it Joseph or Jesus who is the source of all the good that we see? And if Jesus is the source, then the question becomes, Will Joseph lead us closer or farther away from Jesus?

Can both churches be true: the LDS church and the historic Christian church? Joseph says no, according to the voice he says he heard from God. And while we may disagree with Joseph as to which church is false, we both can agree that both churches cannot be true. Jesus is the one true object of our faith. Our disagreement is over who he is, and which way is the true way to reach him. And that disagreement is not trivial, but fundamental.

The central issue of faith, which this book was written to examine, is: To what extent do the facts from the lives of Jesus and Joseph lead us to believe that they can be trusted to lead us to the real God? The fruits of their followers do not resolve the issue. The fruits of these men's lives are crucial to guide us as to whom we should follow.

# CHAPTER 14

# WHO IS MOST WORTHY OF OUR TRUST?

Jesus and Joseph – two extremely important men to know! One makes a claim on our lives that only God can make. The other claims to be the only prophet who can reliably point us to Jesus. And while we cannot know them as completely as someone living in their day could know them, and we are forced to rely on the historian's tools to know what we know, what we know gives us enough evidence to draw the conclusions we must draw in order to make the faith decisions we must make about them.

## The Results of Our Search

We have demonstrated that the historical Jesus found in the Gospels is not a wishful invention or a whitewash job. While his earthly life was far removed from us in history, it is not so far that we cannot know what we really need to know about him. We don't need to know trivia such as what he looked like: how tall was he, how dark was his skin, or how long was his hair. We do need to know: **1.** He "committed no sin; no deception was on his lips" (1 Peter 2:22*), to quote his closest earthly confidant, who was in the unique position to know the honest truth. Jesus lived what he preached, and his word could be trusted. **2.** He spoke and acted as if he was God. **3.** He rose from the grave, which confirms all that he said and did.

This Jesus is real and is worthy of our trust. It is my hope that our conclusions on our search for the historical Jesus will lead us to follow this Jesus wherever he leads and at all costs, regardless of what we may conclude in our search for the historical Joseph. If Jesus is a hoax or is unworthy of our trust, Joseph becomes at best a promoter of fantasies, because he claimed to represent this Jesus. And to repeat what I said in chapter 1, I am determined not to take away anyone's faith in Joseph, unless they are on board with Jesus, no matter what the results may be on Joseph.

It is unlikely that unrecorded or undiscovered evidence about Jesus ever existed that would have produced a different result. We have little if any reason to fear that words or acts of Jesus have been covered up or changed that would discredit his character or trustworthiness, or that any other part of the truth about his life has been fabricated in order to deceive us. Jesus is not an imposter, or the tragic object of a global misunderstanding (as depicted in the plots of *Life of Brian* and *Jesus Christ Superstar*).

That was the fear that suddenly struck me when I was on my internship preparing to become a pastor. After studying Joseph and his church for over four years, I was convinced that the claims about Joseph and his message were false, and that the truth had been covered up, honest people believed what they were told, and the rest was history. But then I asked myself, "How do we know that didn't happen to **us?**" How do we know that Jesus' resurrection was not a hoax that was inflicted on us by a similar story of runaway deception, undetected until the evidence disappeared? I struggled with this fear for months, but finally I came to grasp the historic bedrock on this all-important question, which I have described in chapter 4.

I cannot prove the truth about Jesus in a test tube, but the historical Jesus is worth betting our earthly life and our eternal destiny on. God has given us enough historical reason to do this, that we need not resort to blind faith.

The historical Joseph raises difficulties for faith that are not easy to resolve. And we don't need to listen to the dirt spread by his enemies. We have the evidence of his own words and of his closest friends and confidants. What we have, we must weigh with care. But when we arrive at factual conclusions, we must decide whether we can trust what Joseph said about the revelations he claims to have received from God.

Joseph tells us that he was visited by angels. So does Muhammad. These claims may be true, or not. But both cannot be telling us the truth about the same God. And even if they did see angels, it does not mean those angels were from God. Paul warns the Galatians, "But even if we, or an angel from heaven, preach any other Gospel to you than the one we preached to you, let him be accursed." (Galatians 1:8) The apostle John warns, "Beloved, do not believe every spirit, but test the spirits, whether they are of God; for many false prophets have gone out into the world." (1 John 4:1) Heavenly messengers are not guaranteed to come from God.

How do we test the spirits? We test the word of any spirit or prophet against what God has already revealed in the scriptures we have, as Paul's audience did in the synagogue at Berea (Acts 17:11). If Joseph claims to point us to the true church of Jesus Christ, we must cross-check his word against the historical Jesus of the canonical Gospels. Spirit must be checked by facts, as best as we can determine them, lest we be misled by the wrong spirit.

Part of our task in this book has been to examine the facts we have about Joseph's life and see if they authenticate his claim to be the prophet God authorized to restart his true church. Does Joseph pass the 1 Peter 2:22 test? Unlike the case for Jesus (whose claims were loftier), we do not expect perfection from Joseph. We merely expect enough consistency for us to put our trust in him. We also have a right to expect that there be no "guile" (deception) found in his mouth. Whatever inconsistency or deception we may find, we must weigh carefully as we decide whether we believe his claims to speak as God's authorized representative.

For me, Joseph's deceptive translation of the Book of Abraham is conclusive evidence that he was not the prophet he claimed to be. For others, the fact that Joseph deceived his wife Emma and his followers about his plural marriages disqualifies him. For others, his teachings about eternal progression and the plurality of gods are unacceptably problematic.

Some point to what appear to be false prophecies, such as the building of the temple in Independence, Missouri (*Doctrine and Covenants* 84:1-5), or that David W. Patten would go on a mission with the eleven apostles "into all the world" in the spring of 1839 (*Doctrine and Covenants* 114:1-2 – he died in the fall of 1838). Or there is Joseph's prophecy before the Nauvoo City Council, as recorded in his journal, and printed in *Millennial Star* 22, no. 29 (1860): 455: "I prophecy by virtue of the Holy Priesthood vested in me in the name of Jesus Christ that if Congress will not hear our petition and grant us protection [from local mobs] they shall be broken up as a government and God shall damn them. There will be nothing left of them, not even a grease spot."[1] But others can find ways to reconcile these issues with their faith in Joseph.

---

[1] Diary of Joseph Smith, December 16, 1843, in *American Prophet's Record*, 432. The prophecy is shortened to end at the word "government" when it is reprinted in *History of the Church* 6:116. Joseph makes a similar prophecy on May 6, 1843: "I prophecy in the name of the Lord God of Israel, unless the United States redress the wrongs committed upon the Saints in the state of Missouri and punish the crimes committed by her officers that in a few years the government will be utterly overthrown and wasted, and there will not be so much as a potsherd left for their wickedness in permitting the murder of men, women and children, and the wholesale plunder and extermination of thousands of her citizens to go unpunished." (*History of the Church* 5: 394)

Our eternal future hangs on whether we correctly assess who these men are and where they lead us. Based on what we know about these two men, we must decide whether Joseph can be trusted to lead us to Jesus, or whether we must turn away from Joseph in order to know the truth that sets us free that can only be found in Jesus.

If we follow Joseph, and he proves to have been false, if he leads us to the wrong God and the wrong way to reach God, we are in as much eternal jeopardy as we would be, if we follow the historic Christian Church and it proves to be as wrong as Joseph said it was. But there are many who belong to Joseph's church who actually believe what the historic Christian Church teaches about God and how to reach God. For them, there is hope, even if they have been following the wrong prophet. But how does that hope become the blessed assurance of salvation?

## Joseph's Way to God: Can We Do It?

Joseph offers us an unattainable hope of reaching the Celestial Kingdom through obedience to all of the laws and ordinances of the LDS gospel. We see it at the top of the official LDS Articles of Faith. After declaring that humans "shall be punished for their own sins, and not for Adam's transgression," Article 3 says, "We believe that through the Atonement of Christ, all mankind may be saved, by obedience to the laws and ordinances of the Gospel."

According to the Articles of Faith, salvation is conditional. We must obey. We must be worthy. And what if we fail? In chapter 13, we saw how much the prophet Spencer Kimball says we must do to obtain forgiveness. And how perfectly must we obey? 2 Nephi 25:23 says the standard is "all we can do."

In Joseph's system, how can we ever know that we've done "all we can do"? For those who strive to reach God and to avoid the eternal suffering of what Jesus calls "outer darkness," Jesus warns us that the standard is: perfection. "Be ye perfect, even as your Heavenly Father is perfect." (Matthew 5:48, KJV) "For I tell you that unless your righteousness exceeds that of the Pharisees and Sadducees, you shall by no means enter the kingdom of heaven." (Matthew 5:21*) The Pharisees had high standards: obey the 623 commandments in the Law of Moses, plus the 800 pages of rules they added to that Law. That's a high standard. Jesus puts the bar even higher! Jesus puts the bar sky-high, for those who try to save themselves by their own goodness.

The apostle Paul understood exactly how high that standard was. For new believers in Galatia who had been sweet-talked into believing that they could obey their way to God, Paul writes, "For as many as are of the works of the law are under the curse: for it is written, Cursed *is* every one that continueth not in all things which are written in the book of the law to do them." (Galatians 3:10, KJV) James the brother of Jesus also understood how high that standard is: "For whosoever shall keep the whole law, but offend in one point, has become guilty of them all." (James 2:10*) God's laws are a package deal. It only takes one weak spot to break a chain, it only takes one pinprick to pop a balloon, and all it takes is one sin to make any one of us an outlaw in the sight of God.

Let's imagine that we've never committed any of the sins listed on the New Testament sin lists such as Mark 7:21-22, Galatians 5:19-21, and 1 Corinthians 6:9-11. That alone would be an impressive track record of obedience! But if we go beyond those lists and measure ourselves by the Sermon on the Mount, the Greatest Commandment (Deuteronomy 6:5), the Love Commandment (John 13:34), and Paul's definition of love in 1 Corinthians 13, we will see just how impossibly high God has set the standard, for those who try to reach God by obedience.

Take, for example, the Greatest Commandment: "You shall love the Lord your God with all your heart, with all your soul, and with all your might."* Who can honestly claim to always love God wholeheartedly? Or what about Jesus' command, "Love one another, as I have loved you?" How can we possibly equal the self-sacrificial love that

Jesus has shown to us? If our salvation depends on how well we obey these two priority commands from God, we are toast.

If God judges us by how well we love one another, what does that look like? The answer may be found in 1 Corinthians 13:4-8*: "Love is patient, love is kind. It is not jealous, it does not brag, it is not conceited, it does not act shamefully, it does not seek its own way. It is not easily provoked, it does not keep a record of wrongs, it does not rejoice over wrongdoing, but rejoices in the truth. Love bears all things, always has faith, always has hope, always endures." Who can honestly say, "That's me. That's how I live. That's how I treat everyone"?

Or see what Jesus teaches in the Sermon on the Mount: "Whosoever is angry with their brother [or sister] without a cause shall be in danger of the judgment, whosoever shall say to his brother [or sister] *Rēqa* [Empty-head] shall be in danger of the Council [the Jewish Supreme Court], and whosoever shall say *Moron!* [that's the Greek word he uses!] shall be in danger of the hell of fire." (Matthew 5:22*) Or what about his teaching that sexual sin is not just in the bed, but also in the head (Matthew 5:28)? Or what about Jesus' teachings not to retaliate (Matthew 5:39), or his teaching to love our enemies (Matthew 5:44)? All this and more is what Jesus has in mind in this passage where he says at the end of the chapter, "Be ye perfect, even as your Heavenly Father is perfect."

## So What's the Good News That Can Save Us?

Jesus and his apostles give us a sky high ethic. How can we ever meet God's standard of perfection? There is only one alternative, if we wish to spend forever with a holy God. Salvation must either be earned by obedience, as Joseph taught, or it else comes as a totally free gift from God.

Paul gives us some glorious Good News: we obtain the forgiveness of sins purchased by Jesus on the cross, not by good works, not by obedience, but by grace! In other words, God gives salvation as an undeserved gift, and all we can do is reach out and receive it in faith.

Where does Paul say that? He says it in a passage that became the heart of my testimony of faith: "For it is by grace that you are saved, through faith; and that is not of yourselves, it is the gift of God, not by works, lest anyone should boast." (Ephesians 2:8-9*) As a teenager, I tried to earn my way to God, but I never felt like I had done enough, even though I would have been worthy to enter an LDS temple. I went to my pastor to ask him how I could be sure that I have done enough to be saved. His answer was this verse about grace. When he explained that grace means favor that we cannot earn or deserve, the lights came on for me. Finally, I understood that what Jesus did on the cross was enough to take away my sins and put me right with God forever. This was Good News that has revolutionized my relationship with God. That's my testimony!

The apostle Paul is overflowing with the Good News of God's grace! He tells us in Colossians 1:22 that what Jesus has done is enough to make us "holy and blameless and irreproachable" in God's sight. Imagine the joy of knowing that! Jesus actually makes us "perfect." Hebrews 10:14* says, "For by a single offering he has *perfected* forever those who are being sanctified." And Hebrews 10:10 makes it clear that "those who are sanctified" does not mean those who have earned it, but simply anyone for whom Christ has taken away all of their sin. What Jesus did on the cross was enough to make us "perfect" forever in the sight of God!

Twenty-nine times Paul talks about being "justified." That is courtroom language which means that Jesus has "put us right" with God. He has literally made us "righteous." Romans 5:1-2*: "Therefore, since we are *justified* by faith, we have peace with God through our Lord Jesus Christ, by whom we also have access to this grace in which we stand." Paul says in Galatians 2:16 (KJV) that we never could have done this for ourselves: "for by the works of the Law shall no flesh be justified." In other words, no one can make themselves righteous by doing what God commands, because none of us can do enough.

Paul writes in Romans 6:23 (KJV), "For the wages of sin is death, but the gift of God is eternal life through Jesus Christ our Lord." Paul says that sin earns a paycheck that none of us want to collect, but God gives eternal life as a free gift that we can never earn or deserve; all we can do is receive it in faith.

Where did Paul get all this? He got it from Jesus, from the Gospel of Luke, where we find Jesus' parable about the Pharisee and the Tax Collector (Luke 18:9-14). A story where a tax collector is the hero meets the criterion of dissimilarity: it does not fit either the Judaism of Jesus' day or the early church. The Pharisee prays to God that he treats people fairly and honestly, he lives by the law of chastity, he practices self-denial, and he tithes every cent of his income, while the tax collector grieves over how badly he's sinned against God, beats himself, and prays, "God, be merciful to [literally "atone for"] me, a sinner!"

The shocking punch line is where Jesus declares that it was not the Pharisee, but the slimy tax collector (!), who went home "justified," that is, "made righteous" in the sight of God. Luke says that Jesus told this story for people "who trusted in themselves that they were righteous." Here is Jesus' clearest teaching about grace: God's mercy is not for those who trust in their own goodness, but for those who know they cannot save themselves. Without this message of grace, without Jesus' atoning sacrifice that takes away every sin we've ever done, Jesus' teaching becomes a law we can never obey.

Jesus is not some figure from the past who gave us burdens too heavy for us to carry, but who then leaves it to us to save ourselves. He has completely removed the barrier of sin between us and God. Jesus says, "You shall know the truth, and the truth shall set you free." (John 8:32*)

Jesus alone makes us worthy! He alone can save us! We could never save ourselves.

Will you choose to place your faith entirely in Jesus and what he has done to take away all of our sin, along with hundreds of millions (Protestant, Catholic, and Orthodox) who believe in the God found in the Nicene Creed? Or will you choose to follow Joseph, who leads to a very different God and a different way? From all that you now know about the historical Jesus and the historical Joseph, who is most worthy of your trust?

I testify to you that the historical Jesus, whose Church has never been extinguished on earth, is the only One who is worthy of our trust. He alone can make you holy, pure, and faultless in God's sight. And all you can do is reach out and claim what he has done for you in faith.

# SELECT BIBLIOGRAPHY

Alexander, Thomas G. "The Word of Wisdom: From Principle to Requirement." *Dialogue: A Journal of Mormon Thought* 14, no. 3 (Autumn 1981): 78-88.

Blomberg, Craig L. *Jesus and the Gospels: An Introduction and Survey.* 2nd edition. Nashville: Broadman and Holman, 2009.

Bock, Darrell L. and Robert L. Webb, eds. *Key Events in the Life of the Historical Jesus.* Grand Rapids: Eerdmans, 2010.

Brown, Raymond. *The Death of the Messiah. From Gethsemane to the Grave: A Commentary on the Passion Narrative in the Four Gospels.* 2 vols. New York: Doubleday, 1994.

Brodie, Fawn M. *No Man Knows My History.* 2nd edition. New York: Alfred A. Knopf, 1977.

Bringhurst, Newell G. "Elijah Abel and the Changing Status of Blacks Within Mormonism." *Dialogue: A Journal of Mormon Thought* 29, no. 2 (1996): 109-140.

Bush, Lester E. "Mormonism's Negro Doctrine: An Historical Overview." *Dialogue: A Journal of Mormon Thought* 8/1 (1973): 11-68.

Bush, Lester E. "The Word of Wisdom in Early Nineteenth-Century Perspective." *Dialogue: A Journal of Mormon Thought* 14, no. 3 (1981): 46-65.

Bushman, Richard Lyman. *Joseph Smith: Rough Stone Rolling.* New York: Vintage, 2005.

Church of Jesus Christ of Latter-day Saints History Department. *Saints: The Story of the Church of Jesus Christ in the Latter Days. Volume 1: The Standard of Truth, 1815-1846.* Salt Lake City: Intellectual Reserve, 2018.

Compton, Todd. *In Sacred Loneliness: The Plural Wives of Joseph Smith.* Salt Lake City: Signature Books, 1997.

Cranfield, C. E. B. "Some Reflections on the Subject of the Virgin Birth." Pages 151-165 in Cranfield, *On Romans and Other New Testament Essays.* Edinburgh: T. and T. Clark, 2001.

Faulring, Scott H., ed. *An American Prophet's Record.* Salt Lake City: Signature Books, 1989.

Hobson, G. Thomas. "*Aselgeia* in Mark 7:22." *Filologia Neotestamentaria* 21 (2008): 65-74. Online at https://www.bsw.org/filologia-neotestamentaria/vol-21-2008/.

Hobson, Tom. "Historicity: Does it Matter?" *Presbyterian Outlook*, Part I: 191, no. 23 (2009): 10-11; Part II: 191, no. 24 (2009): 17-18; Part III: 191, no. 26 (2009): 16-17. Online: www.pres-outlook.org.

Hobson, Tom. *What's on God's Sin List for Today?* Eugene: Wipf and Stock, 2011.

Hurtado, Larry W. *Lord Jesus Christ: Devotion to Jesus in Earliest Christianity.* Grand Rapids: Eerdmans, 2003.

Jessee, Dean C. "The Early Accounts of Joseph Smith's First Vision." *Brigham Young University Studies* 9, no. 3 (1969): 275-294.

*Journal of Discourses, by Brigham Young, President of the Church of Jesus Christ of Latter-day Saints, His Two Counsellors, the Twelve Apostles, and Others.* 26 vols. Liverpool: 1854-1886.

Licona, Michael R. *The Resurrection of Jesus: A New Historiographical Approach.* Downers Grove: IVP Academic, 2010.

Marquardt, H. Michael, ed. *The Joseph Smith Egyptian Papers.* Includes Joseph Smith's *Egyptian Alphabet and Grammar.* Salt Lake City: Utah Lighthouse Ministries, 2009.

Meier, John. *A Marginal Jew: Rethinking the Historical Jesus.* 5 vols. New Haven/London: Yale University Press, 1991-2016.

*Nauvoo Expositor.* Nauvoo, IL: 1844.

Petersen, LaMar. *Hearts Made Glad: The Charges of Intemperance Against Joseph Smith the Mormon Prophet.* Salt Lake City: LaMar Petersen, 1975.

Pratt, Orson. *The Seer.* Reprint of the 1853-54 periodical. Salt Lake City: Utah Lighthouse Ministry, n.d.

Prince, Deborah Thompson. "The Ghost of Jesus: Luke 24 in Light of Ancient Narratives of Post-Mortem Apparitions." *Journal for the Study of the New Testament* 29, no. 3 (2007): 287-301.

Smith, Joseph Jr. *History of The Church of Jesus Christ of Latter-day Saints.* Introduction and notes by B. H. Roberts. 7 vols. 2nd rev. ed. Salt Lake City: Deseret, 1971.

Smith, Joseph Jr. *The Holy Scriptures – Inspired Version.* Independence: Herald Publishing House, 1991.

Tanner, Jerald and Sandra. *The Changing World of Mormonism.* Chicago: Moody, 1980.

Tanner, Jerald and Sandra. *Mormonism: Shadow or Reality?* Salt Lake City: Modern Microfilm, 1972.

Walters, Wesley. *New Light on Mormon Origins From the Palmyra (N.Y.) Revival.* LaMesa: Utah Christian Tract Society, 1967.

Wilson, John A., Richard A. Parker, et al. "The Joseph Smith Egyptian Papyri." *Dialogue: A Journal of Mormon Thought* 3, no. 2 (Summer 1968): 67-105.

Wood, Wilford C., ed. *Joseph Smith Begins His Work.* 2 vols. Salt Lake City: Wilford C. Wood, 1962.

Wright, N. T. *The Resurrection of the Son of God.* Minneapolis: Fortress, 2003.

CPSIA information can be obtained
at www.ICGtesting.com
Printed in the USA
LVHW100155071219
639735LV00005B/11/P

9 781400 329014